The Social Agreement

Jode Himann

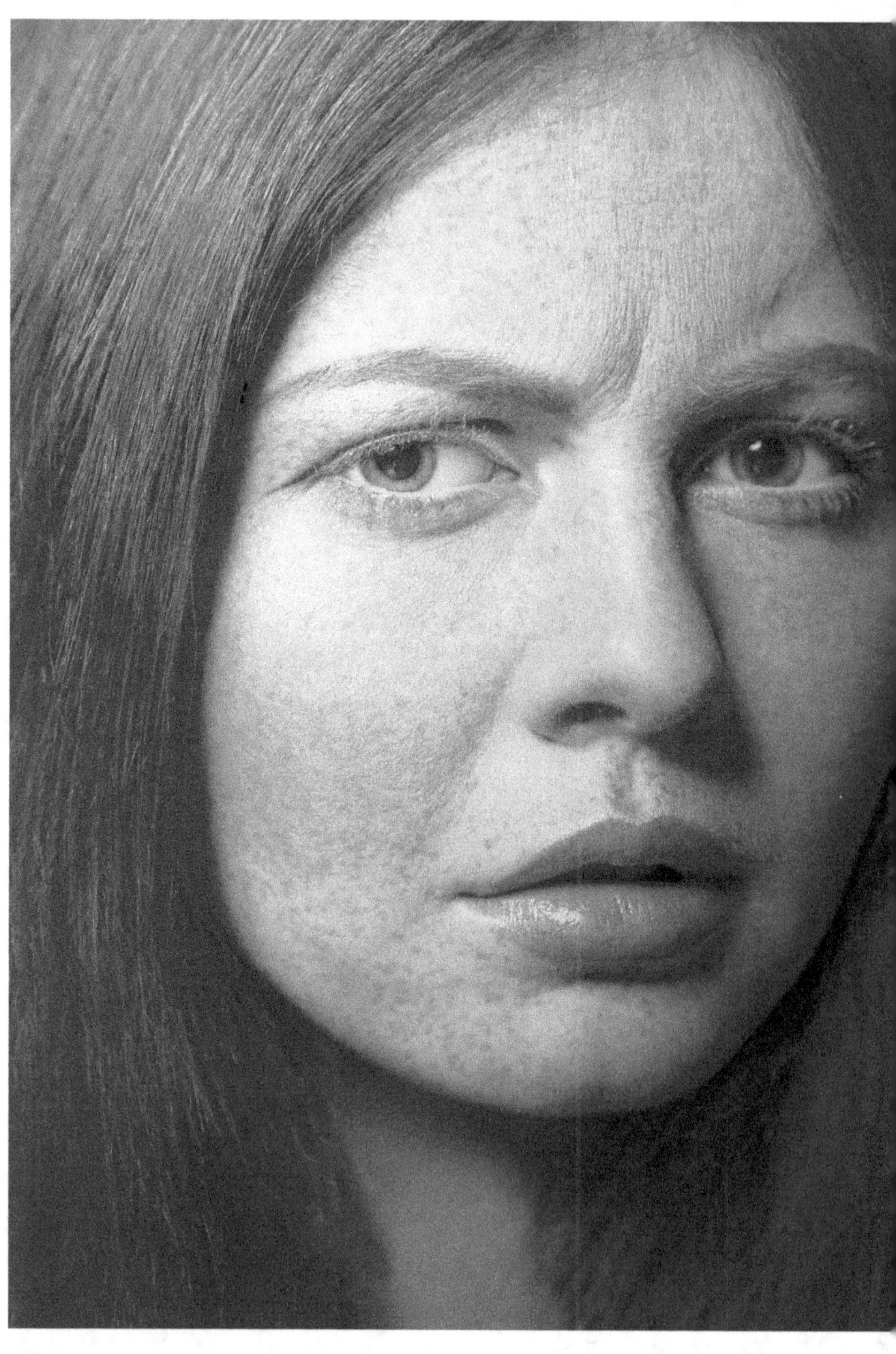

CONTENTS

"Total revolution of consciousness and our entire social, political and economic system is what interests me, but that's not on the ballot" RUSSELL BRAND

INTRODUCTION

The idea that humans possess fundamental rights, shared equally by all citizens of the world, forms an important pillar of contemporary political philosophy. Persistent use of the term "human rights" in media indicates that the concept has gained a firm foothold in mainstream, cultural consciousness. Despite near universal acceptance of innate human rights for citizens, news broadcasters and publishers find no shortage of human rights violations, committed by governments and corporations around the world. Prominent philosophers such as Locke, Mill, Hegel and Hobbes have written on the subject of human rights. The consideration of human rights, and subsequently political rights throughout history by leaders of thought, indicate the importance of the subjects. However, when atrocities committed by the Nazis came to light at the end of the Second World War, the international community discovered that the United Nations Charter did not adequately define the "rights" which it committed to global citizens. The UN's "Universal Declaration of Human Rights," ratified in 1948, remedied the situation by clearly defining the rights of individuals in a series of Articles. In particular, Article 7 of the document states that "all are equal before the law and are entitled without any discrimination to equal protection of the law". Since 1948, the concept of political equality has been held up as an essential protection against governmental abuses of power, which include the indiscriminate

killing of citizens by governments. Renowned political theorist
Robert Dahl stated that Democracy (our social contract) was
designed to prevent such tyrannies. The human will to live (or
fear of death), then, inspires the logic behind the supposedly
a priori equality of human rights. Basing a political philosophy
on the individual will to live (as the essence and fundamental
reason for a social contract) legitimizes democratic structures
and celebrations of human diversity. In the early days of Darwin's
theory of natural selection, altruism (generosity) was viewed as the
one critical anomaly which could not be satisfactorily explained by
a theory based purely on competition and survival of the fittest.
Evolutionary psychologists and game theorists (in particular
the influential thinker Robert Axelrod) have since demonstrated
how collaboration and cooperation promote increased group
and individual fitness. According to Axelrod's findings, human
society follows in the evolutionary footsteps of other, more
primitive species that also leverage altruistic behavior and social
contracts for direct benefit to the group and indirect benefit for
the individual. And, thereby, improve chances of survival for the
individual and for the group.

Humans, like other animal species, possess natural survival
instincts. Through our brief evolutionary history, we have
uncovered social cooperation as the optimum survival strategy.
Compelling arguments in modern Leadership studies claim
that democratic systems are the best governance systems for
large, modern societies (Slater & Bennis, 1990). The seminal work
of Warren Bennis, founder of the field of Leadership studies,
argues that traditional, autocratic management structures are ill
equipped to manage the rapid rate of change associated with
the modern era. The best groups—no matter the situation—are
those that communicate well (giving a voice to each member),
that work together effectively (realizing and developing individual
talents) and that harvest value from the competencies of all team
members. In other words, Democracies. An individual's interest
in the group's ability to perform and profit extends from the
individual will to live. A group's ability to perform depends on
the strength of its communication mechanisms and its level of

respect and care for all members of the community. Democratic structure acknowledges and balances the individual will to live with the needs of the group.

Hence, Slater & Bennis argue that Democracy—which is inherently egalitarian, pluralistic and liberal—is the only system of human organization capable of effectively governing a modern, technological society, given an accelerating rate of change. They also find tremendous value in citizens and societies who can continually learn about the conditions that shape their existence and who can refine group dynamics to respond to those ever changing conditions.

Principles for governing large societies also apply to governance of smaller groups. The importance of meaningful belonging, open communication and equality, then, ought to inform the structural organization of businesses and the teams that comprise businesses. As Slater and Bennis put forth (in the article already quoted), companies benefit from Democratic governance in the same way that nations do. Corporations are not only the drivers of technological innovation and growth, they are microcosms of civilization. As such, why do we tolerate such a profound gap between ethics and philosophies in the public and private sectors? One attempt to integrate politics into corporations include James Whitehurst, president of Red Hat (the world's leading open-source software vendor) champions the role of Democratic values in the workplace. Whitehurst, in his book *The Open Organization: Igniting Passion and Performance*, focuses on the principle of meritocracy as a core value for Democratized companies. In a meritocracy, any employee (whether a CEO or a new hire) has equal opportunity to contribute their voice. This openness, Whitehurst argues, is a benefit to the employee and to the organization as a whole.

Pursuant to fundamental values of equality and rights, this paper presents an argument for the benefit of opening up workplaces to voting and for including, in that process, options for voluntary vote delegation systems. The argument relies on two axioms.

Firstly, that a Democracy must give citizens a right to vote on decisions that will affect the collective. This familiar idea requires relatively little discussion. In a Pure Democracy (also known as a Direct Democracy), the citizenry determines policy initiatives and other public decisions directly, not through the votes of elected representatives. Direct voting is closer to Democratic ideals than Representative Democracy but is not always practical for large, geographically dispersed or technologically limited populations. The second axiom: Democratic voters ought to have the right to delegate their votes to others (and to revoke said delegations), as they see fit. A number of lines of reasoning recommend this second, less familiar axiom. First, it preserves the voting power of those who are otherwise unable or unwilling to vote (due to time pressures or limitations of knowledge, for example). Such individuals may know of others who possess values similar to their own and who are also known to be well-informed on the relevant issues. Transferring votes allows all citizens to have their values accurately reflected, even those who choose not to cast a ballot themselves. Thus, the second axiom is supported by the notion that a society is less Democratic when only group members with ample free time or sufficient education can cast meaningful votes. Further, while delegation may be seen as a transfer of power from voters to representatives, one may also view delegation as a transfer of information (about how to vote). Implementing a "proxy" option into the structure of democracy would strengthen the nodes in the existing social network. Structural Deep Democracy is a phrased coined by Mark Rosst and potentially an apt description of theoretical result of offering a proxy option in our social contract. The specific implementation of a proxy voting social network outlined in this paper would be able to harvest value and information from a group quantifying the qualitative value, Any rejection of the second axiom, then, would suggest that organizations ought to restrict the flow of information, to their own determent.

Taken together, these two axioms indicate that a voluntary delegation system is more democratic than either a traditional representative system or a direct voting system that precludes delegation. If one accepts these axioms, what line of reasoning would justify the choice of a traditional representative system over a system that allows for voluntary delegation? Traditional Democracy is highly vulnerable to the criticism that it produces arbitrary and/or biased results whenever voters are not fully informed of the issues at stake. How might a voluntary delegation system perform under the same conditions? The following essay offers an analysis of voting practices in the context of imperfect information and proposes systemic reforms so badly needed, to bring Democracy in-line with the needs, challenges and benefits of the digital age.

"*The duty of youth is to challenge corruption*" KURT COBAIN

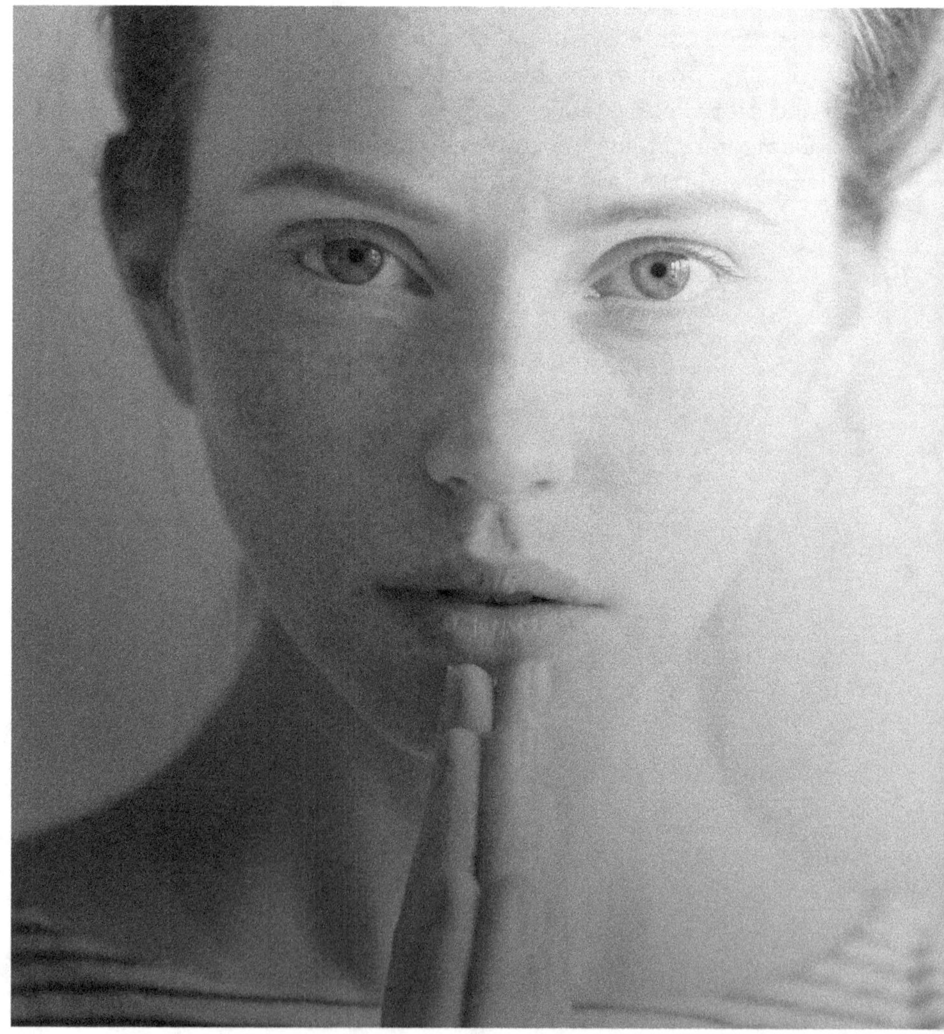

MODERN DEMOCRACY

G lobally, modern governments vary greatly in their practices and guiding philosophies. New Zealand, for example, adjudicates its Democracy by principles and methods different from those which generate Democratic beliefs and concepts in countries such as Angola or France. Societies govern themselves in different ways because each nation possesses a unique culture and history and faces unique economic, social and ecological challenges. These endlessly variable challenges demand unique approaches to governance. Many nations select the Democratic model, because it offers unmatched adaptability and is ultimately customizable to specific needs. In spite of this, Democratic systems are far from perfect. No lesser a man than Winston Churchill famously quipped, "Democracy is the worst form of governance, except for all the others". Perhaps no Democracy in history has managed included all members of society. Historically, racial groups, women, slaves and even those who do not own property have been excluded from so-called public "Democracies." To take a more recent example, Canada only granted the vote to women in 1919; today, we still do not include youth as voters and the Conservative party has (in 2015) revoked the right to vote from Canadians who choose to live abroad. A further weakness of Democratic governance: policies result from compromises, which should seek the greatest good for the greatest number (while protecting the rights of minorities). For this reason, Democratic systems cannot meet all the diverse and often competing demands placed upon them by their citizenry. Given these points of vulnerability, trust in government can run very thin, in response to actual or perceived dysfunction within systems of governance. Perceived dysfunction combines with large group voting size to produce voter apathy. Today, many people feel that public Democracy no longer serves the needs of the people. The reasons for this are many and diverse but it has become clear that today a number of factors threaten the relevance and the future of Democracy. The authors of this paper, however, do not share a fatalistic vision for governance in the future. Rather, this paper seeks to address reforms that will return governance to the people it would serve.

A systematic analysis of the diverse threats to the viability of modern Democracy may reveal a common root dysfunction. All modern democracies have a built-in sociological Achilles Heel that requires explicit investigation. Anthropological research—particularly the work of Dunbar, Bernard and Killworth—has demonstrated an upper limit to the number of players in a meaningful social network. "Dunbar's Number," named after the anthropologist Robin Dunbar, first appeared in his 1992 seminal paper, "Neocortex Size as a Constraint on Group Size in Primates." Dunbar identified the number 148 (usually rounded to 150) as the largest number of people with whom one can have meaningful and reciprocating relationships. Dunbar began with the premise that the modern day human's neocortex has its origin 250,000 years ago, in the Pleistocene epoch. He then searched anthropological and ethnographic datasets to determine the size of hunter-gatherer tribal populations. Dunbar's number (150) poses an inherent problem to the idea of meaningful and reciprocating engagement in modern Democracies, whose participants often number in the tens or hundreds of millions. All the various forms of civil disengagement, which recent anthropological and sociological research has revealed, can be traced back to our flagrant defiance of Dunbar's Number.

The Ancient Greek philosopher Plato measured the maximum number of citizens that could form a functioning democracy at 5300. Democratic representatives in Canada, especially those serving at the federal level, attempt speak for too many people. Dunbar's number indicates that these representatives cannot effectively listen or speak to even the majority of opinions held within their ridings. As a result, many citizens believe the political system is broken and trust in our government systems is on the decline.

In contemporary Democratic systems, disfranchisement felt by citizens can be attributed, in large part, to problems with the ways governments provide and receive communication. Citizens commonly view governmental communications as authoritative monologue, instead of healthy dialogue. An elected representative cannot effectively represent their constituents without hearing and responding to their concerns and ideas. Citizens do not have the sense that they have direct access to their representatives, in part because emails and phone calls are channeled through an intermediate layer of assistants, secretaries and public relations professionals who acts as representatives of the representative. If citizens who voice their concerns—through contacting representatives or through civic protest—witnessed immediate and direct government response, voter apathy and other forms of civic disengagement would not pose such an urgent problem. But the sad reality is that voices of ordinary citizens are ignored in the current political process; only professional lobbyists, backed by significant campaign contributions, have reliable access to politicians. As an example, the US government is well known for corporate lobbying. The total amount spent on campaigns by all candidates for Congress in 2010 was $1.8 billion. If the vast majority of Americans, those without the necessary funds to access Congresspersons, believe their participation in Democracy will not count for much, they will choose to direct their attention elsewhere (Lessig, 2011). The hallmark of honest, well-intentioned dialogue is clarity and directness. In contrast, the bureaucratic nature of contemporary governance leads communication to become jargon-heavy, double-speak, evasive or simply non-representative. In addition to the language of government, entrenched privileges of powerful politicians give the impression that the Democratic process is not open to all citizens.

At one time, the federal government of Canada regularly posted new bills for debate and even new laws on-line and asked its citizens for input. This process not only improved legislation, it improved citizen engagement in the legislative process. Today, the foundational framework for the government of Canada's communications is no longer transparent, robust and clear. The federal government hides its plans and its legislation from the public. Debate, engagement and even expert opinion are actively suppressed. All this leads to citizens who distrust their government. Even the most open governments struggle to encourage participation, as a citizen's engagement depends, in part, upon his or her leisure time and political literacy, not only on a willingness or desire to participate. How difficult, then, to raise participation levels, given the current political climate in Canada.

A study of "Trust in Government" in Canada (Nano, 2011) found that a sizeable portion of respondents expressed distrust in government leadership. The survey found that enforcement of government regulations, work in the public interest, procurement of government contracts and appointment of non-elected officials all scored less than 5, on a scale of 10. Many of these problems stem from poor communication with citizens. Without transparent and effective communications between government and citizens, the public will gain insufficient knowledge about the qualifications of people applying for public positions, the status of projects that affect them or contract procurement processes. Improving communication frameworks, stratagem and platforms will improve the functioning of governmental systems and restore a measure of trust and pride to civic life. This could result in greater participation in the political process, better governmental policy and stronger communities (including reduction in crime rates and better use of public monies).

In a culture where super PAC's, billionaire donors and lobby groups appear to control the political process, individuals cannot help feeling that their voices fall upon deaf ears. Effecting change within a disempowering framework requires extra efforts—such as collecting signatures for petitions, sending letters and emails to representatives or arranging personal meetings with elected officials. Democracy rewards those who communicate with their fellow citizens and elected representatives in these ways. A general distrust of the political system, however, increases the cost of communication and discourages all but the most passionate of individuals from voicing their dissent and rallying fellow citizens to their cause.

To effect sustainable change, it is not enough to treat the symptoms of these problems. We must arrive at the root cause. Often, the most difficult problems are those in which the root cause is hidden in plain view. When we take a step back and consider how modern Democracies operate, one obvious fact emerges: elected officials represent constituencies of at least many thousands of people. Is such representation fair and feasible, in a modern Democracy? How can one elected representative hear, interpret and respond to the thousands of voices within his or her constituency, when Dunbar's number sets the limit of meaningful and reciprocating relationships at 150? Continuous population growth only exacerbates this problem further. Representational Democracy depends on leaders who cannot know the needs and desires of their constituents. This leads to errors, misunderstandings and confusions which combine to produce distrust and disengagement.

In order for modern, Representational Democracies to work more effectively for the overly-large populations that they serve, the problem of citizen-government communication must be addressed. Society must find a way to recover authentic, reciprocal communication stratagem. And while the real strength of Democracy lies in its capacity for self-improvement, it is unfortunate that many Canadians feel that their governmental systems have moved beyond the point of repair. Improvements become very challenging in an atmosphere in which citizens are have lost hope. To bridge the trust gap, governments must not only speak but also listen; citizens must not only listen but also speak and offer meaningful feedback. Governments must stop the inauthentic and ultimately unhelpful practice of telling the votership only "what they want to hear," while simultaneously acting against public wishes. To repair broken trust, governments must shift efforts from gathering inconsequential, private information through intelligence agencies to listening to the critical opinions that citizens hold.

Digital technology may have an important role to play in counteracting inadequate parliamentary representation. The internet has already revolutionized commerce, entertainment, education and social interaction. Could it also help remove the obstacles that presently constrain citizen-governmental dialogue? The effectiveness of future governments, in the digital age, may depend on the responsibility, adaptability and technological savvy of our governmental communication systems.

Further, one might consider voter apathy as the specter which haunts modern Democracies. Sociologist and author Robert Putman popularized the term "social capital" in his book, *Bowling Alone: The Collapse and Revival of American Community* (Simon & Schuster, 2000). His research brought to light the serious decline in civic engagement in American society, beginning in 1950. This pervasive decline includes not only a drop in voter turnout, attendance at political rallies and public committees. Putman traces civic decline to time spent with family, community, religious groups as well as a weakening of labour unions, parent-teacher associations, women's groups and other volunteer activities (Boy and Girl Scouts, the Red Cross, Lions Clubs and etc). Inspiration for his book's title came from that fact that although more Americans than ever before bowl, fewer and fewer join organized bowling leagues. Putman's research shows that attendance in public meetings plunged by 50% between 1973 and 1994. For Putman, solitary bowling becomes a symbol for the decline in community. Despite diminishing social capital—which undermines the effectiveness of Democracy—prominent sociologists Philip Slater and Warren Bennis argue, in their article "Democracy is Inevitable" (Harvard Business Review, 1990), that democracy remains the most effective form of governance for modern technological societies.

In a modern Democracy, the body populous constitutes the sole sovereign, that exercises political power indirectly through elected representatives. Representative Democracy arises largely from ideas and institutions that developed during the European Middle Ages, the Reformation, the Age of Enlightenment and the American and French Revolutions. No consensus exists among historians and political scientists on the definition of Democracy but equality, freedom and rule of law have been identified as its enduring principles. Contemporary political thinking purports that Democracy has never been fully achieved but that it remains an essential ideal for a world that values equality, human rights and evolving systems of organization. These principles are reflected in the equality of all adult citizens before the law and their equal access to legislative processes. For example, in a Representative Democracy, every vote carries equal weight, no unreasonable restrictions can prevent anyone from seeking political office and constitutions protect the legitimized rights and liberties of citizens. The renown political thinker Dr. Richard Kimber, in his books and articles, asserts that democracy requires three fundamental characteristics: 1) upward control (i.e., sovereignty resides at the lowest levels of authority) 2) political equality and 3) controlling the actions of individuals and institutions through social norms rather than brute force and limiting such actions to those that prioritize upward control and political equality. A further tenant can be added to Kimber's characteristics—the capacity of all voters to participate freely and fully in the life of their society. With its emphasis on notions of social contract and the collective will of all voters, Democracy can also be characterized as a form of political collectivism because it is defined as a form of government in which all eligible citizens have an equal say in decisions that affect their lives. In order to merit the label "modern Democracy," a nation must fulfill some basic requirements. These need to be not only recorded (in a constitution, for example) but must be maintained, in everyday life, by politicians and authorities. These requirements include:

- Guarantee of basic Human Rights to every individual vis-à-vis the state and its authorities as well as vis-à-vis any social groups (especially religious institutions) and vis-à-vis other persons.

X Separation of Powers between the institutions of the state:
Government (executive power), Parliament (legislative
power) and Courts of Law (Judicative Power).

X Freedom of religion, association, opinion,
speech, press and other media.

X General and equal right to vote (one person, one vote).

X Good Governance (focus on public interest
and absence of corruption).

While maintaining these priorities, Delegative Democracy
can be distinguished from Representative Democracy by "the
principle that each voter should have free, *individual* choice of
their delegate—not just a choice among a restricted set of career
politicians—just as we already make a free, individual choice of
our friends". Proponents of Delegative Democracy (or "Liquid
Democracy" coined by a group in Germany) believe that making
individual relationships important to the political process will
restore or improve faith in Democratic governments who adopt
this system. Delegative systems build on the central Democratic
principle that representatives will develop communication and
relationships with their citizens and promote citizen engagement.
Too often, voters face ambivalent choices between impersonal
candidates. That weakness is inevitable in the current state of
Representative Democracy, as creating personal relationships
is time consuming and may rate low on lists of campaign
priorities especially with a group size in the thousands.

In a Liquid Democracy, vote transfers resolve the separation
between voters and politicians, which currently forms a significant
barrier to participation in the Democratic process. Liquid
Democracy leverages existing trust relationships, rather than
attempting to create new ones. A proxy vote delegate will respond
more immediately to the needs of a citizen and will understand
their needs and beliefs better than will an impersonal career
politician who governs across significant distances and massive
populations. In Delegative Democracies, unsatisfied voters can
immediately remove their vote from their trusted delegate,

which can have serious repercussions for political leaders (from city and town counsellors to prime ministers and presidents). Delegates—as opposed to representatives—are held directly accountable to voters. Liquid Democratic systems, then, return our modern conception of governance to the founding principles of Democracy (power emanates from the people and individual political freedom), while correcting for three thousand years of population growth. In Liquid Democracy, delegates must continually work to earn the trust of voters. In order for Democracy to flourish in groups larger than the populations of small Canadian towns (approximately 5000 inhabitants), one must employ robust communication systems to transmit and receive information between representatives and constituents. Those systems must be highly flexible in order to maintain stable relationships within the constituency.

The ground-breaking research of Robert Putman has established that social capital is on a downward spiral. Civic engagement is in rapid decline, public education in civics has been reduced while society has become more concerned with the desires of the individual than with the common good. Perhaps this apparent decline can be partially explained by a shift in community organization that results in new forms of engagement that escape our traditional measures for such activity. The nature of our communities and paths of development remain in a state of flux and theorizing and measurement often struggles to keep apace. However, the decline in voter turn-out seems to validate the opinion that societal connections have been undermined by the rise of individualism. While the communication gap between politicians and citizens widens, the populace enjoys greater connectivity, thanks to digital platforms. The social networks that exist within and across immigrant populations and the general population may well be one of the most significant trends that Canadian society will face in the coming decades. Governments and other forms of leadership (business executive boards, for example), ought not to fall behind in advancing the development of our social contract to synchronize with what is necessary to support individual freedom and group success.

Democracy and the Corporate Sector

We can already see how some groups have engineered around the failing legacy democratic infrastructure. One development that may have helped undermine citizen trust and engagement with government in recent history is the continual rise of monetary influence in Democratic politics. The line between public and private interests has all but disappeared, given staggering campaign finance and the proliferation of Crown Corporations. As government comes to more resemble business, savvy business leaders perceive an opportunity to Democratize the workplace (by enforcing employee preferred party support). Many contemporary thinkers believe that western Democracy has entered a period of crisis. The crisis manifests in low levels of public participation in governance and rapidly declining voter turn-outs (Putman, 2000).

Since the emergence of modern capitalism, politics and governance have become increasingly shaped by financial capital and powerful private interests. Citizens may rightly feel that their own voices go unheard in the political process, drowned out by the better-funded interests of multi-national corporations, professional lobby groups and wealthy individuals who determine the nature of political campaigns and public policies. Because the corporatization of government has created a sense of political hopeless and alienation, this paper speculates on the empowering effects that may come from the inverse process: increasing democratic practice in the private sector. Critics of capitalism find money incompatible with the principles of Democracy. While that idea may hold for parliamentary systems, adopting Democratic structures may strengthen the world of business. Entrusting one's employees with greater roles in decision making holds the potential to create stronger decisions, boost work-place morale and ultimately increase profits for corporations. This is in contrast to today's political climate, where the centralization of political power—which benefits the wealthiest individuals and corporations—has led to a disaffected, and potentially revolutionary, electorate.

The primary relationships of an individual are those maintained with family, friends, neighbors and work colleagues. Strong ties describe the relationships of an individual with relatives and friends; connections with acquaintances (such as neighbours or colleagues at work) constitute weak ties. People with varied network of relationships report higher levels of satisfaction and happiness (Lelkes, 2010; Helliwell, 2008) as well as strong mental health (Williams et al.,1981). However, people with poor health, particularly mental health, have been reported to have significantly smaller social networks (Halpern, 2005). Personal relationships are important for individual wellbeing, but can also have positive outcomes for firms and organizations and at the level of community (Halpern, 2005).

Improving our ability to understand and foster social capital will require major advances in our research and policy approaches. Conventional wisdom recognizes that diversity of participation can lead to greater innovation. Innovation arises when difference is brought together in meaningful or valuable hybrid forms. In the language of social capital, effective organizations must mix bridging capital (linking external factors to the core group) and bonding capital (strengthening links within the core group). New information, insight and opportunities arise from effective bridging capital, which may then transform practices conducted by the core group. This principle applies to any group, from small business to multi-national corporations and from individual societies to online, global communities.

"What are we passing down to the next generation? Are we passing down our cultural wealth? Or are we passing down our liabilities?" JANE ROLAND MARTIN

VOTING, PSYCHOLOGY AND COMMUNICATION

In its current state, Democracy does not encourage self-review of governmental communication and voting systems, although industry has proven that self-review produces high levels of efficiency in the corporate sector. Rather, citizens are asked to integrate their changing thought—and possibly aberrant opinion—into a static, governmental structures. Perhaps the safety of comfortable paradigms in a rapidly changing world outweigh the value of updated policy change. Our existing systems of governance leave little room for emotive relationships, dialogue or dissent, despite the fact that campaigning politicians often evoke emotion and a spirit of dissent in their speeches. In 2005, Princeton psychologist Alexander Todorov noted that voters' selections had more to do with subjective perceptions than with objective, political facts (Todorov, 2005). Given this democratic environment, methods and content of communication demand close study.

There are many subtle influences on the way we think and how it affects our decision making. Some of the influences are primitive, like how we react when we identify and meet a potential mate. Others are environmental, like the influence of food or allergies. Some others are in our DNA design. Our combination of influential variables make us who we are. Being aware of these variables will help us make better group decisions.

Voters most often base their decisions on qualitative impressions, such as competence, rhetoric and affability. Todorov suggests that such impressions could derive from considerations of facial features alongside more reliable (or more scientific) forms of data and logic. Todorov's study indicated that election results might, in large part, come from what Nobel-winning psychologist Daniel Kahneman calls "fast, unthinking judgment" or what psychologist Nalini Ambady calls "thin-slice judgment: the ability to make any number of social judgments from a seconds-long experience" (Ambady, 2010). Like Ambady, Todorov found that citizens make political decisions—such as who they will vote for—very quickly and that increased time for consideration made little impact on their choice. He also found that participants in his study could better judge a candidate's competence and qualifications in the absence of images of the candidate. Without access to quality information about candidates, and without meaningful communications with politicians, individual voters rely on subjective perceptions, in place of data. Emotional reactions to campaigns act as poor replacement for real knowledge about policy platforms and political history. Contemporary citizens face diverse demands on their time and conducting individual research into pertinent political debates is simply not feasible for many voters. Citizens govern the government by selecting a number of its members. However, this responsibility is not supported by allotted or paid time and resources to research candidates. In populated jurisdictions, especially, the likelihood of meeting candidates in person is very low. Assessing candidates for office in a given election cycle, then, is largely a matter of guesswork, in the current state of Democracy. Liquid forms of voting strengthen exchanges of information about political issues by optimizing personal networks, through which private considerations become public conversations.

Psychological researchers use the term "algorithm aversion" to describe the phenomenon whereby humans prefer traditional or instinctual knowledge to the solutions and predictions provided by computer intelligence. For example, while Google Maps can often provide the most direct travel route, a user may feel that by relying exclusively on Google's service, they will miss out on local knowledge (shortcuts or scenic routes) that lies beyond the reach of computer programs. Despite risks that can arise from human error—wrong turns, misdiagnosis and profit-loss, for example—many people insist upon maintaining human agency in governmental and corporate decision making. Researchers Dietvorst, Simmons and Massey have found that humans forgive occasional errors on the part of human decision makers but come to distrust computer algorithms more easily, based on even lower rates of error (Dietvorst et al, 2015). In computer programs for chess, route-mapping, medical diagnosis and other areas of analytics, decisions made by complex computer algorithms prove more reliable than those made by humans. In light of this, why do we continually distrust computer intelligence? Why do we have "algorithm aversion"? The primary cause is that most humans do not understand the way in which computers analyze information to arrive at predictions and solutions.

The paper "Algorithm Aversion: People Erroneously Avoid Algorithms After Seeing Them Err," published by Dietvorst, Simmons and Massey, is the culmination of various experiments in the psychology of human-to-computer trust. In one of the experiments, participants reviewed admissions data and predicted the performance of students who had been accepted into an MBA program. Participants, who would earn money for accurate predictions, were also given the option of allowing an algorithm program to make guesses on their behalf. Some participants could review their own accuracy as they progressed, some were shown the accuracy of the algorithm and some could access neither or both of these measurements. Participants who knew the exact predictive performance of the algorithm were found less likely to delegate their predictions to the computer program, even if they also knew their own results (which were invariably less accurate than those produced via the algorithm). These findings held across a variety of experiments, despite the introduction of increasingly accurate algorithm programs by the researchers. Participants in further experiments were found more trusting of other peoples' predictive power than that of computer programs, even of those programs whose results they knew.

When asked to explain their distrust of algorithms, participants most commonly stated that "human forecasters were better than the [computer] model at getting better with practice [and] learning from mistakes" (Dietvorst et al, 2015). Algorithms can improve also, of course, although human understanding of computer intelligence clearly lags behind recent innovations. Dietvorst, Simmons and Masseys's experiment found that faith in human judgment is grounded in perception of our ability to learn, adapt and improve. In other words, our ability to evolve. Exposure to the accuracy of human/algorithm predictions did not reduce "algorithm aversion" but Dietvorst, Simmons and Massey did reduce algorithm aversion by allowing for human-algorithm collaboration. In a forthcoming paper, these researchers will publish results that find participants more willing to delegate their predictions to computer programs if they can also make adjustments to those results, at their discretion. For example, should an algorithm predict that an MBA student will finish in the top 10% of their class (based on admissions data), participants could move that benchmark up or down, by a few percentage points. Even that minor level of collaboration increased the rates at which participants delegated their predictions to algorithm programs. That relatively inconsequential level of input bolstered participants' confidence in computer programs' analytical and predictive capabilities, even when participants could access the algorithm's results and despite the fact that such adjustments invariably weakened the accuracy of the algorithm's predictions. Humans pride ourselves on our ability to learn. Ironically, we seem slow to learn to trust the power of computer analytics.

Digital technology has made contemporary life at once easier and more challenging. One regrettable side-effect of a ubiquitous digital information network is an increasing sense of information overload. With so much information now available, citizens have a difficult time parsing out data relevant to them. As sociologist Robert Putman's studies have firmly demonstrated civic engagement has experienced a radical decline since the 1950s (Putman, 2000). Putman and many others believe that digital distractions drive us away from community participation. We interact with mobile and computing devices individually, at the expense of community interaction grounded in the physical realm. As we sift through a virtual landscape—filled with marketing, gossip and seemingly endless sources of information—investment in political education or community activism suffers. From the 1950's to 1990's, many parents used television to babysit their children; today, tablet computers and mobile phones do this work. Parents can manage children with gadgets more easily in the short term; over the long term, the same parents may find children addicted to video games, screens and social media more difficult to manage than children raised in traditional, social and outdoor environments.

In the digital age, with its multiple streams of information, selecting relevant issues of governance from a sea of noise poses a daunting task. With the Internet of Things on the horizon, even more data streams will emerge, including significant quantities of unstructured, organic data generated by sensors, video, audio, social media and other technologies. For this reason, ascertaining qualities and exchanges of social capital will become even more difficult than today. Society ought to invest in developing consistent formal measurements for intangible value and in studying the relationship between unstructured and structured data. Given a glut of information, we must also consider what effect crossing a maximum threshold of information overload will have. Only rigorous study can reveal and resolve the gap between the extant volume of information and the tools available to assimilate information. Some studies show that information overload leads to poor decision making (Hwang and Lin, 1998).

Five factors contribute to information overload:

- Personal Information: personal qualifications, experiences, attitudes, etc.

- Information Characteristics: information quality, quantity and frequency

- Tasks and Process: standardized procedures or methods

X Organizational Design: organizational cooperation,
processing capacity and organizational relationships

X Information Technology: IT management,
software and hardware capabilities

An overburden of knowledge interferes with the ability to make
rational decisions (Hall, Ariss, Todorov and Phinyor, 2007).

One way to reduce the burden of overwhelming information is to
leverage large groups of people for data processing tasks. The
Wisdom of the Crowd comes to displace isolated individuals,
in the digital age, as a source of value and receiver of trust.
Aggregate responses and findings, produced by groups, have
generally been found equal to or better than those generated
by any individual. The averaging affect produces this increase in
quality: the rightness of a majority view cancels out idiosyncratic
noise associated with erroneous, individual judgments. The
Wisdom of the Crowd may sound like a new term, but the process
itself is far from new. At a country fair in Plymouth, in 1906, a
crowd of 800 participated in a contest to estimate the weight of a
slaughtered and dressed ox. Statistician Francis Galton (who was
present at the fair) observed that the median guess, 1207 pounds,
was accurate within 1% of the true weight: 1198 pounds. Today,
social information sites such as Wikipedia, Yahoo! Answers, Quora,
Reddit and other web resources rely on collective opinion, just as
our society has long trusted in the rightness of trial by jury. Rather
than small juries, employed in courtrooms, todays online juries can
number in the millions of persons. Decisions can now be made
by large and diverse groups, instead of by a single expert, judge
or a homogenous group with shared interests and motivations.
At the same time, social science researchers have uncovered that
group opinions suffer when groups lack independent thinkers
and other forms of diversity (Polavieja and Madirolas, 2014).

Scott E. Page—Professor of Complex Systems, Political
Science and Economics—introduced the diversity prediction
theorem: "The squared error of the collective prediction equals
the average squared error minus the predictive diversity"

(Page, 2007). This formula shows that when the diversity in a group is large, the error of the crowd is small. Page's studies indicate the need for close consideration of the psychological concept of present-day decision making. Psychologists regard decision making as the cognitive process resulting in the selection of a belief or a course of action among several alternative possibilities. Every decision-making process produces a choice that may or may not prompt action. Decision making requires identifying and choosing from alternatives, based on the values and preferences of the decision maker. Decision making is a central activity of business management, although the process itself receives little investigation because influential factors prove so difficult identify and quantify.

Cognitive bias, a deviation in judgment in which inferences are drawn in an illogical fashion, also complicates decision making. Researchers Amos Tversky and Daniel Kahneman established the notion of cognitive bias in their studies of innumeracy (the phenomenon that reasoning capacity degrades when dealing with greater orders of magnitude) (Kahnerman and Frederick, 2002). Although the reality of these biases is confirmed by reproducible research, there are often controversies about how to classify biases or how to explain them. Many biases may result from information-processing rules (i.e. mental shortcuts), called "heuristics," that the brain uses to produce decisions or judgments. Tversky and Kahneman explain human differences in judgements through the concept of heuristics, which provides quick estimates of uncertain occurrences (Baumeister & Bushman, 2010, p. 141). Heuristics simplify computation for the brain but sometimes come at a cost of introducing "severe and systematic errors" (Tversky & Kahneman, 1974, p. 1125). Biases in judgment or decision making can also result from eccentricities of motivation, when wishful thinking distorts beliefs, for example. Some biases have a variety of cognitive ("cold") or motivational ("hot") explanations. And both effects can be present at the same time.

Scholars of psychology have produced no consensus as to whether some biases count as truly irrational or whether they result in useful attitudes or behavior. For example, when getting to know others, people tend to ask leading questions which seem biased towards confirming their assumptions about the person. This kind of confirmation bias has been seen as an example of sociability: a way to establish a connection with the other person. Research on psychological biases overwhelmingly involves human subjects. However, some findings have come from study of non-human animals as well. For example, hyperbolic discounting of certain informational streams has been observed in rats, pigeons, and monkeys.

Biases can be categorized into:

X   Decision making, belief and behavioral biases

X   Social Biases

X   Memory errors and biases

Some of the biases are listed below by various categories. Many of these biases affect belief formation, business and economic decisions, and human behavior in general. What the plethora of biases illustrate is how easily we can be led astray.

The Wisdom of Crowds can produce superior decision making that results from collective processing, thereby balancing and eliminating cognitive biases of individuals. The insight that estimations by groups can be modeled as samples of probability distribution invites comparisons with individual cognition. In particular, it is possible that individual cognition is probabilistic in the sense that individual estimates are drawn from an "internal probability distribution." If this is the case, then two or more estimates of the same quantity from the same person should average to a value closer to truth than either of the individual judgments, since averaging reduces statistical noise within each judgment. This reasoning assumes that the noise associated with each judgment is (approximately) statistically independent. Another caveat is that individual probability judgments are often biased toward extreme values (e.g., 0 or 1). Thus, any beneficial effect of multiple judgments from the same person is likely to be limited to samples from an unbiased distribution. The democratic structure benefits in improved decision accuracy from the variety and number of votes.

One proposed solution to the communication challenges imposed by governmental hierarchies and population expansion is proportional representation. In such systems, the number of elected bodies is proportional to the relative public support for the various political parties and candidates. For example, if 25% of the electorate support a particular political party, then roughly 25% of the seats would be held by that party. In theory, proportional representation ensures minority groups are given a measure of representation proportional to their electoral support. However, recent experiments in New Zealand (with the Mixed Member Proportional representational system) failed, due to unforeseen outcomes. Voter and citizen confidence in government declined under the proportional system of representation because measures intended to mitigate the problem of communicating with a large populace were not commeasurable to the population gap, between those who lead and those who are led. Other solutions to the communication challenges faced by democratic governments, however, are currently gaining attention.

Another proposed solution to governmental communication and confidence challenges is the idea of Liquid or Delegative Democracy. This system re-envisions the relationship between the citizenry and its leadership as a dialogic relationship, one defined by authentic dialogue between the two parties. Proponents of Delegative Democracy promote the idea of a barrierless spectrum, between those with little or no political interest to those empowered to make decisions and introduce laws at the federal level. Liquid Democracy does not rely on the old (or current) system of strict hierarchy between the voter and the vote-seeker. A voter's delegate, in Liquid forms of Democracy, is not a stranger who one evaluates based on their campaigning. Rather, one might choose to pass one's vote on to a trusted friend, colleague or family member. That individual, by acquiring the vote of their fellow citizen, becomes their delegate, a representative to government through the power of their vote. Citizens can communicate with their delegates with a level of directness and dialogue that is precluded by our current system, that of representation. Further, if a delegate is seen to not adequately or ethically represent their fellow citizens, the position of delegate can be revoked with a minimum of effort (in comparison to the effort now required to oust an official from public office: investigations, hearings and political trials). In Liquid forms of Democracy, existing trust networks are leveraged to make governance an extension of community. Further, transparency and ethical behaviour become urgent concerns for delegates whose positions are more direct than remote, more precarious than assured.

Liquid Democracy also incorporates debate and multiple points of view more readily than does Representational Democracy. Rather than relying on an elite few who are nominated to represent a largely voiceless populace, Delegative Democracy enables anyone to become a representative. A delegate can represent just one other person, or hundreds of thousands The number of citizens a delegate represents depends on how many individuals' trust he or she earns. In Delegative Democracy, citizens have a greater amount of choice among views that they can support by bestowing the delegative role. At heart, Liquid Democracy improves faith in governance by developing and leveraging quality relationships (potential and extant) between voters and delegates. Leaders who represent fewer citizens can better hear, interpret and respond to a variety of opinions and needs. Liquid democracy, then, would improve voter confidence by allowing citizens to select the best individual to represent them from their broad communities, not a narrow ballot of officially sanctioned candidates.

Schools of political thought that encourage democratic participation (Westminster, Cellular or Jacksonian Democracies) provoke a common concern: if more individuals obtain power in a Delegative Democracy (albeit diffuse levels of power), more opportunities for political corruption arise. This could lead to an increase, not a decrease, of public disinterest and disgust, as corruption would become more immediate, apparent and perhaps more common. However, it has been demonstrated that corruption can also be detected and dealt with more swiftly and directly in a Liquid Democracy than in a Representational system. Quality relationships form the basis of Delegative Democracies and those relationships are more easily monitored and changed than the traditional relationship between voter and representative. As Delegative Democracy becomes adopted, the value of quality of relationships will start to inform governmental policy and practice in all areas of governance.

The communication practices of corporations, organizations and governments have been the subject of psychological research for nearly a century. Over the past generation and more, psychologists interested in the way organizations communicate have begun to study not only the quantifiable values of communication but the qualitative values as well. The context of organizational communications helps to shape the receiver's interpretation, although context and interpretations prove much less tangible than the content of messaging.
The book *Communication and Organizations: An Interpretive Approach*, by Linda Putnam and Michael Pacanowsky, appeared in 1983 and set in motion a wealth of theorizing about value of qualitative information within organizational communication. This work promoted a diversity research methodologies, alternatives to the statistical analyses that had previously dominated the field. Subsequently, distinctively qualitative data techniques such as interviews, observation, narrative analysis, demographic considerations and communication philosophies have come to play a large role in shaping our ideas about organizational communication. Current and recent research in this field demonstrates that what we communicate cannot be separated from how and why we communicate.

"The intuitive mind is a sacred gift and the rational mind a faithful servant. We have created a society that honours the servant and has forgotten the gift." ALBERT EINSTEIN

EVALUATING QUALITATIVE VS QUANTITATIVE DATA

As in the political realm, communication systems and data analytics support the effectiveness of business enterprise. Corporate leadership makes decisions based on collected information, both quantitative and qualitative. Quantitative data comes in the form of hard numbers: sales sheets, accounting of overhead and profits that detail historical performance and future earnings. Business responds to this kind of information with analysis, measurement and projection. The other stream of information that informs business decisions comes in the form of qualitative data (also known as intangible value), which executives respond to with instinct honed over years of practical experience. This second source of information cannot be measured with exactitude but businesses who neglect intangibles do so at their own peril.

Business leader Warren Buffet emphasizes the criticality and intangibility of qualitative values as follows:

Businesses logically are worth far more than net tangible assets when they can be expected to produce earnings on such assets considerably in excess of market rates of return. The capitalized value of this excess return is economic goodwill. (Buffett, 1983)

On a similar note, Richard Branson addresses the importance of intangible value in the music business, when he says: The music industry is a strange combination of having real and intangible assets: pop bands are brand names in themselves, and at a given stage in their careers their name alone can practically guarantee hit records. (Branson, n.d.)

Buffet and Branson both recognize that the total value of a successful business surpasses its tangible assets. Businesses that value both quantitative and qualitative factors increase their value. By the same token, neglecting intangible factors may devalue a company. Assets that resist quantification—such as Research and Development costs or brand recognition—do not figure prominently in businesses analysis that focuses on the hard numbers of overhead vs. sales. A 2008 study, conducted by Hulten and Hao, finds that formerly excluded, intangible assets represent 40 to 50 percent of the market value of R&D intensive companies in the U.S. Such assets appear significant in explaining the market-to book-value puzzle (Hulten & Hao, 2008). Questioning which values can be measured, or which metric will most accurately determine those values, challenges established notions of political value and social capital. Making a decision, casting ballots or assigning roles are processes of evaluation and measurement on two levels: fact and feel. In a voter's' analysis of options, personal beliefs combine with perceptions of a candidate's fitness (his or her historical performance, competency, lineage, party and background). For some voters, even a candidate's visual appearance, dress and bone structure may affect a voting decision.

Too often, the difficulty of applying a metric to intangible, qualitative values (such as "trustworthiness," "drive" or "charisma") reduces their effect in decision making and shifts the emphasize to variables that can be measured with a greater degree of confidence. At the end of the 19th century, Francis Galton stated "until the phenomena of any branch of knowledge have been submitted to measurement and number, it cannot assume the status and dignity of science" (Galton, 1879). American psychologist James Mckeen Cattell stated that, "Psychology cannot attain the certainty and exactness of the physical sciences

unless it rests on a foundation of experiment and measurement"
(Cattell, 1890). Galton's firm pronouncement was based upon
the work of his predecessors, especially the Medieval scholar
John Duns Scotus and the German philosopher Immanuel Kant.

Science seeks to discover governing principles in nature: structural
operations, attributes and their interrelation (causal or otherwise).
Where only qualitative information exists, science is limited in
its predictive power. If intangible values could be measured,
great advancements in knowledge would follow because
accurate measurements reveal previously unseen patterns of
behavior. That which is not measured often goes unnoticed. An
eye for talents such as imagination and instinct is often gained
through experience, although that talent may go unobserved
because it does not show up in statistics or annual reports.

Unlike scientific realists, operationists view measurement
as a philosophically distinct category of scientific activity.
Because other scientific concepts are defined by measurement,
measurement takes logical priority over other scientific
concepts, in the operationist view. The representational view,
that measurement involves a distinctive relation of numerical
representation, sees measurement as a hybrid of the empirical
and the conventional, raising the issue of the apparently
"unreasonable effectiveness of mathematics in the natural
sciences" (Wigner, 1960) (including politics).When scientists set
about devising practical, standardized procedures for measuring,
it is precisely these real numbers (ratios between unknown
magnitudes and the unit adopted) that scientists attempt to
identify. The most important factor distinguishing measurement
form other methods of scientific inquiry is the context of
application—quantitative attributes and ratios that they sustain.

After the Second World War, new regulations for researchers
emerged in the U.S.A., conditions documented by Schorske
(1997) and Solovey (2004). These new requirements led the
human sciences (psychology, economics and sociology, for
example) to imitate the quantitative rigor of the physical sciences

(e.g., biology, chemistry and physics). Heightened public perception of psychology's laboratory and methodological rigor (the ability to measure quantitative value) maximized funding opportunities under the new, post-war dispensation. New funding policies forced the qualitative methods previously employed by psychological researchers into decline. This shift occurred within a new cultural paradigm that evolved from the Enlightenment period of the 17th century, which privileged quantification and associated hard numbers with objectivity clarity.

If psychology and other qualitative, social science disciplines desire scientific legitimacy, it seems that practitioners must limit their inquiries to quantifiable, objective phenomenon and fact. Today, the desire for illusory objectivity has filtered into many areas of society, including democratic institutions. Attempts to quantify a voter's decision-making process have overshadowed investigations into some of the equally valuable qualitative variables. A particular habit of thought in Western civilization assumes the authority of quantitative over qualitative values. This bias is particularly evident in instances where quantitative conceptions determine important choices, even when direct experience shows such valuations to be extremely limited, if not entirely false. The impossibility in creating tangible quantifiable metrics for our group qualitative values have hindered democratic group strength and continues to do so. One economist attempt to measure the qualitative (intangible) value in the US economy resulted in a 3 trillion dollar asset measurement. Social capital was not included in this study but would be a considerable additional value. Our inability to quantify this value means that we cannot harness or harvest our qualitative value and it is then lost.

SOCIAL CAPITAL AND TRUST

Social capital, as a concept, is a relatively new term defined as the value derived from the total of one's social networks and community activity. Social capital, then, includes personal and professional relationships (in physical or virtual form), social networks and support, civic engagement and belonging or membership to specific groups (from fraternities and societies to boards and neighbourhood watch groups). Social capital also includes the benefits generated through these connections and actions. In the early days of social capital research, the concept was applied exclusively to the social potential of an individual (in characteristics such as charm, sociability, affability and usefulness to neighbours). More recently, the influential sociologist Robert Putman has reframed social capital into an attribute of collectives. He focuses on social norms and trust relationships as producers of social capital. For Putnam, social capital benefits the individuals who possess it as well as the wider community of which they form a part. Social capital is germane to our present considerations, because of its positive contribution to a range of societal factors that sociologists measure, such as personal well-being and crime rates. Increased social capital leads to benefits on many levels: individual, community, regional, national and global. Social capital has been recognized as a driver of economic growth because an increase in social capital results in greater economic efficiency.

"Social Capital has been recognized as a driver of economic growth, resulting in greater economic efficiency" (Putnam, 2000, and 1993; Fukuyama, 1995). At a macro-level, it is likely that higher levels of trust and cooperative norms reduce transaction costs, thereby driving productivity (Putnam, 2000, and 1993). At an individual level, people with wider social networks are more likely to find employment (Aguilera, 2002), to progress in their career (Lin, 2001) and to earn high wages (Goldthorpe et al. 1987). The importance of social capital was recently acknowledged by the Bank of England governor Mark Carney, who stated that "prosperity requires not just investment in economic capital, but investment in social capital" (Carney,2014). World Bank efforts to estimate the "true wealth of nations" suggest that intangible capital, made up mainly of human and social capital, represents around 60-80 per cent of true wealth in most developing countries (World Bank, 2006). However, social capital stocks are not presented as monetary values in this article. Although some researchers have tried to estimate the value of social capital assets as a proportion of total wealth (Hamilton and Liu, 2013), social capital differs from natural and human capital as it is a broad concept, based largely on interpersonal relationships.

The question of measurement in the social sciences forms an important consideration for any inquiry which attempts to quantify social capital. In fact, the subject of measurement in psychology and the social sciences has been surrounded by a great deal of controversy. Today, measurement in the social science is notably different from ideas of measurement in other science disciplines (Michell, 1997). Psychologist Joel Michell writes that "even though quantitative psychologists (by whom I mean those who either theorize about or attempt to measure psychological quantities) hypothesize that their attributes are quantitative and, so, commit themselves to the concept of scientific measurement, the definition of measurement actually endorsed by most of them is radically different". Curiously, while science has applied techniques of measurement to every conceivable phenomenon in the galaxy, very few scientists have pursued measurement itself as an area of investigation.

Social capital is an aggregate concept that addresses not only interactions with a group but also individual behavior, attitude and predisposition. As alluded to above, the problem of measuring or even estimating trust in a social network is a very interesting and challenging one. Trust, as an aspect of social capital, remains both undefined and poorly understood. If psychological attributes such as trust cannot be quantified, then the field of social science cannot benefit from the power of mathematical analysis that has proven so valuable in so many other fields of science. The Merriam Webster dictionary defines trust as the belief that someone or something is reliable, good, honest, effective, etc. The online psychology dictionary defines trust as confidence a person or group of people has in relying on another person or group In a social context, trust typically refers to a situation characterized by the following relationship. One party (the "trustor") consents to rely, in good faith, on the future actions of another party (the trustee). The trustor, then, transfers personal control to the trustee. Since trust is based in assumptions about the personal character and competence, trust always contains an associated degree of risk. Always present in ideas of trust, one finds the opposite: the possibility that the trustee could fail and bring about disappointment or harm (distrust). The trustor's expectations can only be validated or dashed by experiencing or witnessing the results of the trustee's completed action.

In the social sciences, subtleties of trust relationships remain the subject of ongoing research. In sociology and psychology, the degree to which one party trusts another is understood as a measure of belief in the honesty, fairness or benevolence of the other party. Trust and confidence are two closely related terms in sociology, however, confidence is perhaps a more appropriate term than trust, to indicate levels of belief in the competence of another party. A failure in trust can be forgiven more easily if it is seen as a failure in competence, not as a failure of honesty. Dishonesty destroys trust and produces suspicion. It was Warren Buffet who said, "it takes twenty years to build a reputation and five minutes to ruin it" The level of trust an individual is ready to commit depends upon their past experience as well as their projected expectations.

In economics, trust is associated with reliability in transactions. High levels of trust and reliability (i.e., confidence in a person's abilities) reduces emotional stress and saves time for the trustor. Without trust, each of us would complete necessary tasks ourselves, suffer emotional stress and create additional processes to ensure that others meet obligations. From another perspective, trust can be considered a heuristic rule which allows the trustor to accomplish a task with minimal effort, thanks to confident delegation. Without the aid of this heuristic, trustors would often face unrealistic levels of effort to complete basic tasks. That is why modern Democracies rely on the value of many intangible qualities, such as trust. Variables such as innovation, relationships and trust are of intrinsic value to groups yet seem to resist quantification and, thereby, escape the attention of leadership. Unless qualitative values can be quantified, they are likely to be neglected factors in decision making. This omission in priorities and analysis relegates the essential value of qualitative elements to latent value. Developing an accurate measurement of social capital would unlock this vast potential, enabling qualitative data to contribute enormously to all aspects of society. The future health of Democratic systems relies on correctly identifying and valuating intangible assets.

Trust also functions as an economic lubricant. Trusting relationships reduce overhead costs and efforts that would otherwise be necessary to support and monitor untrusted persons. Hence, trust allows transactions to flow more freely, thereby reducing the cost of transactions between parties. Trust, then, frees up efforts and so enables new forms of cooperation and generally furthers business activities, employment and prosperity. Trust is an essential component of social capital and this has inspired research into the processes of trust creation and distribution. In a society of trusting individuals, economic activity will be a greater and economic welfare higher than in a society in which trustworthiness is lacking (Tisdell, 2008).

Effective social norms, developed by a robust civil society, serve to regulate behaviour, lessening requirements of law enforcement and judicial punishment. The extent to which social capital is embedded in social structures determines the extent to which it can contribute to the public good (Narayan,1998). Conversely, when only powerful and tightly knit groups possess and exploit social capital, society suffers. Such groups harm society by prioritizing individual gains over the common good. Abuses of power of this kind come from individuals who do not feel accountable to the population as a whole; their actions accelerate social inequality and instability. Elitism and the centralization of power result in corruption in government, nepotism and cronyism (Evans, 1989; Mauro, 1995; World Bank,1997).

While personal or corporate bank accounts store economic capital, social capital resides inside relationships and imaginations. Although we all intuitively understand social capital—in that we all exercise, waste, develop and lose it every day—the concept's intangibility makes it difficult to measure, analyze and discuss. To possess social capital, a person must relate to others in the community. It is the relationship to these others, not the individual in question, which is the true source of social capital (Portes, 1998; Deepa Narayan and Michael F. Cassidy, 2001). Proponents of Delegative Democracy believe that by leveraging existing trust relationships and social capital, vote delegation can help increase trust in government.

Citizens in a Liquid Democracy have direct access to the structure of the society they inhabit and would logically be more likely to engage in cooperative endeavors (than citizens of a representative system), setting in motion a "virtuous circle" through which trust promotes cooperation and cooperation promotes trust (Putnam 1993). Astute study of history reveals, as an inevitable lesson, that compliance with societal expectations is inefficient when based on fear of authorities, rather than on internally regulated and positively enforced norms. Citizens of a democracy rely on the government to protect them from lawlessness, not to achieve collective purposes (Gamson 1968; Putnam 1993; Uslaner 1994). A too often neglected duty of governance and citizenship is to question what which areas of life require state intervention and which do not.

Social capital is a core idea used by a broad range of researchers in the social sciences, ranging from urban planners to health policy workers. Despite the concept's measurement challenges—and because of its importance to social inclusion, crime, and mental health—social capital is a growing area for research and research application. The white paper from the 2013 University of Waterloo Roundtable on Social Capital stresses the criticality of social capital in determining and shaping our communal endeavors (Friesen, 2013). The concluding remarks of this white paper point to three approaches to the difficulty of measuring social capital. Friesen writes:

There is a great deal of work yet to be done on social capital. If Elinor Ostrom and T.K. Ahn are right, measuring the phenomena will occur over decades or longer. We must not be dissuaded by the difficulty of the task, the complexity of the field, or the complications inherent in attending to this rich social phenomenon. Globally, we are experiencing human migration at unprecedented scales. Economics, cultural shifts, technological intrusions, resource scarcity, massive health issues and many other deep factors will both shape and express themselves through changing fortunes in social capital. It is critical that efforts to understand these changes empirically grows along with the challenges. There are three possible approaches that might be taken:

- **Wishful Thinking:** notionally support the active academic conversation to enable it to move forward with irregular interactions at a policy level. As the academic conversation matures and deepens, something will eventually jump the gap and find its way into policy – the longer attention span of academics will at some point carry the day;

- **Direct Engagement:** actively organize to ensure

that the process above is pursued intentionally and richly through conferences, funding strategies, rich multiple exploratory projects, development of an ecosystem of supporting institutions, organizations and stakeholders, and effective education programs that include community level organizers;

X **Abandon:** do nothing and accept that the conversation has evolved and moved in other directions such that formal social capital pursuits are drawn on as historical resources with a certain limited utility but not a substantive future.

Friesen, in his sarcasm, rejects the first and third approaches to the problem of social capital. The full story of social capital, as a critical aspect of the social sciences, ought to inform our solutions to significant governance and policy needs. Community leaders of all stripes must attend to the relationship between confidence and participation. Many studies of voter turnout and democratic participation find a positive correlation between beliefs about the responsiveness of political authorities, or external efficacy, and civic engagement (Rosenstone and Hansen 1993; Brady, Verba and Schlozman 1995). Social networks of civic engagement are at the very core of social capital (Putman, 1993) and so strong networks enable strong communities: those that can solve collective action problems by breeding cooperation and facilitating coordination.

Improving Democracy requires enhanced trust of other people—citizens and politicians, those who are known and unknown to us. Assurance facilitates cooperation, whenever one feels relatively confident about the incentives and abilities of other actors. Trust then spreads through a community, by reinforcing norms of reciprocity and self-interested cooperation (Putnam 1993). These norms then become a part of the community's social capital, allowing individuals to make inferences about the intentions of others, even when direct or absolute knowledge about them is unavailable. A general atmosphere of trust creates a positive feedback effect. When we put trust in others, social capital increases. Increased social capital ultimately heightens the quality and quantity of economic transactions. In the current and uncertain economic climate, an increase in public trust could have wide-scale impact and inspire not only increased confidence in democratic arrangements but also inspire positive structural reforms of same.

Psychological studies demonstrate that negative moods heighten people's sense of danger and threat (Marcus et al. 1995). The strongest antidote to emotional distress (caused by periods of economic turbulence or political uncertainty) is the support of long standing trust relationships. In their paper, "Individual-Level Evidence for the Causes and Consequences of Social Capital," John Brehm and Wendy Rahn find a positive and reciprocal correlation (a "virtuous circle") between civic engagement and social trust (Brehm & Rahn, 1997). Their study finds that civic engagement is more likely to increase trust than vice-versa. Brehm and Rahn also find that the correlation between engagement and trust is a precarious one—degrading either engagement or trust creates a "vicious circle" more easily than increased engagement or trust leads to a "virtuous circle." Political and business leaders should find these results troubling because confidence is the currency in which they trade. The independent effect of interpersonal trust on confidence suggests that even improved performance of government may not be sufficient to obtain substantial levels of confidence from the public. Confidence in institutions, indicated by high levels of civic engagement, has been shown to bear a strong connection with interpersonal trust in fellow citizens (Brehm & Rahn,1997). In summary, social capital lies at the very heart of our political and social institutions. Social capital plays an intrinsic role in society that must be integrated into policy and decision-making at all levels of society.

"Obviously I don't vote as I believe democracy is a pointless spectacle where we choose between two indistinguishable political parties, neither of whom represent the people, but the interests of the powerful business elites that run the world." RUSSELL BRAND

HARNESSING AND HARVESTING VALUE

The complex phenomena of social capital will be of much less use to us if we are unable to measure it. At some point in the future, social capital may turn out to refer to a key aspect of social physics that underpin both wider societal dynamics and person-to-person interactions and relationships.

Measurement of social capital also ensures that the phenomena are attended to in policy and public good decision making processes. Consistent measure also allows for comparison over time and from place to place. It is possible to develop, a suite of social capital instruments calibrated so that research can be meaningfully generalized.

A designed social metric would also have to synchronize with the fundamental problem of citizen-to-government communication and requires a structural analysis of decision making in the age of the internet. If Democracy is premised on governments making decisions on behalf of the populous, how digital technology could facilitate decision making, the inclusion of a social metric and communication becomes a critical question for political scientists and community leaders. This section of the essay considers the structure of how society interacts with digital technology and how to best integrate a scale into this interaction.

Stanley Smith Stevens, the preeminent Harvard psychologist, was a leading figure in developing a theory of measurement, unique to the social sciences. He first introduced his theory of measurement in a 1946 article, which appeared in the journal *Science*, entitled "On the Theory of Scales of Measurement." His theory was further codified in the influential 1951 *Handbook of Experimental Psychology*. Stevens defined measurement as "the assignment of numerals to objects or events according to some rule" This definition contested the established definition of measurement, guiding other scientific pursuits, as the ascertainment of the weight, size, temperature (attributes, in brief) of some object or event by comparison to a standard unit. For example, one modern definition, aligned to the physical sciences, conceives measurement as the numerical estimation and expression of the magnitude of one quantity relative to another (Michell, 1997). To understand Stevens' peculiar definition of measurement in the human sciences requires an understanding of the social context in which his definition arose (as well as of the culture of science during the early twentieth century). Stevens's definition of measurement was a response to the British Ferguson Committee whose chair, A. Ferguson, was a physicist. The British Association for the Advancement of Science appointed the committee in 1932, to investigate the possibility of quantifying sensory events. Stevens belonged to a school of thought called Logical Positivism which attempted, in the tradition of Decartes, to exorcise all unverifiable ideas from science. Stevens practiced what was known as operationalism. In fact, Stevens contributed a definition of operationalism to Dagobert D. Runes' 1942 *Dictionary of Philosophy*, defining it as "the doctrine that the meaning of a concept is given by a set of operations" On this basis, objects and events under investigation will appear to conform to our operational definitions of them. An example of the limitations of this view is E. G. Boring's famous definition of "intelligence" as "what intelligence tests test" In his lab work, Stevens discovered that the most direct way of measuring the perceived intensity of sensory stimulus—such as light, sound, smell, or electric shock—was simply to ask people to assign a number value to their perceived experience. Participants of his studies assigned numbers to experience without perceived limits on the scale (such as "between one and ten"). Neither did Stevens offer choices between limited number sets or specify the units for numerical values. Sensations measured in this uncontrolled fashion displayed an orderly relationship to the physical magnitude of sensations, a phenomena that is now named Steven's Power Law, in his honor. Steven's Power Law is an *exponential* relationship which equates subjective sensation with the quantifiable, physical magnitude (stimuli) raised to a constant power. The exponent in the equation acts as a unique constant, representing the particular kind of stimulation such as a particular taste to the palette, brightness of a light or loudness of a sound. Stevens characterized and measured countless stimuli using this power law. Today, the human sciences still teach Steven's four levels of measurement to introductory psychology classes. Stevens' Power Law is not limited to physical or ratio measurement but includes rankings and interval scales as well. While Stevens worked to legitimize physical experience by developing methods of quantifying it, today the question remains whether subjective attitudes and beliefs could be directly quantified (i.e., expressed as a ratio of some fixed unit).

Innovating communication and decision making systems begins with a review of how organizations gathering substantive qualitative and rigorous quantitative data. Because social impact and sociability are so difficult to measure, such qualitative factors are often overlooked by leadership. This issue highlights the tensions that exist between the dominant cultural narratives of economic progress and the sometimes less visible and less easily quantified importance of social well-being. While technology can assist with some aspects of environmental sustainability, human behavior (at individual and collective levels) will profoundly shape our future, just as it has shaped our past (Owen, 2010).

Social dynamics are complex and non-linear; they cannot be fully understood through rational interpretation, unchecked assumptions or single variable analyses. Ostrom and Ahn argue that: "Social capital, with only a decade of history of empirical applications and attempts at measurement, does exhibit serious problems of measurement. But the concept is firmly placed in the context of major empirical and theoretical puzzles related to economic and political development. It would not be wise at all to dismiss the concept on the ground that it is difficult to measure (Ostrom & Ahn, 2003, p. XXXIV).

Currently, social capital is measured using a standard set of questionnaires. The "amount" of social capital in a given community is then extracted from the results of the questionnaire. Different countries have different benchmark questionnaires that establish the value of the social capital. Some examples of the Social Capital Measurement Guidelines include SOCAT (World Bank), International Social Survey Program, Canadian Index of Wellbeing, Social Capital Index, Social Capital Measurement Tool (SCMT) as well as many others.

These have been selected as representative of the various ways that social capital measurement is understood depending on context, scale, purpose, and scope. The 2005 Franke Report reflects the rudimentary outlines of a social capital taxonomy that has not realized its full potential in subsequent years.

During the Social Capital Roundtable, one participant noted that qualitative motivations capture the attention but that only quantitative results inspire people and organizations to invest. A consistent metric, currently missing for most qualitative values, allows for determinations of effectiveness over time. Such a metric, if discovered, would help determine which inputs or changes lead to positive results. If no useable tools emerge for measuring or understanding social capital, its long-term value and impact will be minimized. The 2005 Franke report, which is little known even among scholars and policy development leaders who are working in, on and around the phenomena, is a good example of the difficulty in translating ephemeral concepts into concrete language. Translating that report into terms that resonate with the current social and policy climate is the only way to inspire funding (both financially and intellectually) projects investigating measurement of qualitative value.

Qualitative values seem to resist measurement, in part, because individuals approach values (like trust) from highly individual perspectives. However, the same could be said of supposedly "hard numbers." One thousand dollars does not have consistent value across economic strata or geographical boarders, for example. Individual perspectives come to shape interpretations of fact, opinion, context and application of information. Further challenge presents itself in that social capital value changes as a group or organization matures. When the group is young and small, social capital is essential to success. The group matures then it is less so. It follows that we should be very careful and conservative in the approach to creating a metric, so that it would be agreeable to a wide range of perceptions and situations. We should start from two basic premises:

✗ Value exists in social capital and trust.

✗ In every group and situation, social capital
   has a synchronized relative value.

 Like social capital, many systems can usefully be represented as networks or graphs—collections of vertices joined in pairs by edges. Examples include the Internet and the world wide web, citation networks, social networks, and biological and biochemical networks of various kinds. Although an old and well established branch of study in mathematics and sociology, research on networks has in recent years attracted significant attention from members of the physics community as well, who have successfully applied a variety of physical ideas to the analysis and modeling of these systems . Most of the networks that have been studied in the physics literature have been binary in nature; that is, the edges between vertices are either present or not. Such networks can be represented by (0, 1) or binary matrices. A network with n vertices is represented by an $n \times n$ adjacency matrix A with elements $A_{ij} = \_ 1$ if i and j are connected, 0 otherwise. However, as has long been appreciated, many networks are intrinsically weighted, their edges having differing strengths. In a social network there may be stronger or weaker social ties between individuals. In a metabolic network there may be more or less flux along particular reaction pathways. In a food web there may be more or less energy or carbon flow between predator-prey pairs. Edge weights in networks have, with some exceptions, received relatively little attention in the physics literature for the excellent reason that in any field one is well advised to look at the simple cases first (unweighted networks) before moving on to more complex ones (weighted networks). On the other hand, there are many cases where edge weights are known for networks, and to ignore them is to throw out a lot of data that, in theory at least, could help us to understand these systems better.

A weighted network is a network where the ties among nodes have weights assigned to them. A network is a system whose elements are somehow connected (Wasserman and Faust, 1994). The elements of a system are represented as nodes (also known as actors or vertices) and the connections among interacting elements are known as ties, edges, arcs, or links. The nodes might be neurons, individuals, groups, organisations, airports, or even countries, whereas ties can take the form of friendship, communication, collaboration, alliance, flow, or trade, to name a few.

In a number of real-world networks, not all ties in a network have the same capacity. In fact, ties are often associated with weights that differentiate them in terms of their strength, intensity, or capacity (Barrat et al., 2004) and Horvath (2011). On the one hand, Mark Granovetter (1973) argued that the strength of social relationships in social networks is a function of their duration, emotional intensity, intimacy, and exchange of services. On the other, for non-social networks, weights often refer to the function performed by ties, e.g., the carbon flow ($mg/m^2/day$) between species in food webs (Luczkowich et al., 2003), the number of synapses and gap junctions in neural networks (Watts and Strogatz, 1998), or the amount of traffic flowing along connections in transportation networks (Opsahl et al., 2008).

By recording the strength of ties, a weighted network
can be created (also known as a valued network). Below
is an example of such a network (weights can also
be visualized by giving edges different widths):

Exploring the information that weights hold allows us to
further our understanding of networks. In social networks,
strong ties are often found among socially embedded
individuals (Granovetter, 1973; Panzarasa et al., 2009).In
fact, Simmel (1950) argued that a strong tie cannot exist
without other indirect ties (weak and strong). Strong ties
facilitate change in the face of uncertainty (Krackhardt,
1992), reinforce obligations, expectations, and social norms
(Coleman, 1988), and promote the transfer of complex and
tacit knowledge by sustaining individuals' motivation to assist
one another (Hansen, 1999; Reagans and McEvily, 2003).

One of Granovetter's (1973) major findings is the idea that
novel and explicit information is more likely to flow to
individuals through weak ties than through strong ones. An
individual's friends tend to move in the same circles, and
therefore are likely to receive the same information that the
individual already possesses. Conversely, acquaintances
are likely to know people that the individual does not, and
thus receive more novel information. If this information is
explicit or codified, it can easily be transferred from the
acquaintance to the individual (Levin and Cross, 2004). In
light of these findings, the measures that scholars typically
apply to study networks should be sensitive to tie strength
and capture the difference between strong and weak ties.
This will ensure that the full richness of the data is retained.

A better way to analyse weighted networks would be to
redefine and generalise current methods to explicitly take
weights into account. Currently, only a small set of measures
have been generalised (Freeman et al., 1991; Newman, 2001).
For example, Newman (2001) generalised Freeman's (1978)
closeness measure by applying a method from computer

science to define the distances among nodes (Dijkstra, 1959). The generalised methods would aid the analysis by removing the bias resulting from the subjective choice of the cut-off.

Some of the types of mathematical models used include generalizations of degree and eigenvector centrality, to the more complex, such as the proposal of a new algorithm for detecting community structure in weighted networks. A weighted network can be represented mathematically by an adjacency matrix with entries that are not simply zero or one, but are equal instead to the weights on the edges:

$$A_{ij} = \text{weight of connection from } i \text{ to } j. \tag{2}$$

For example:

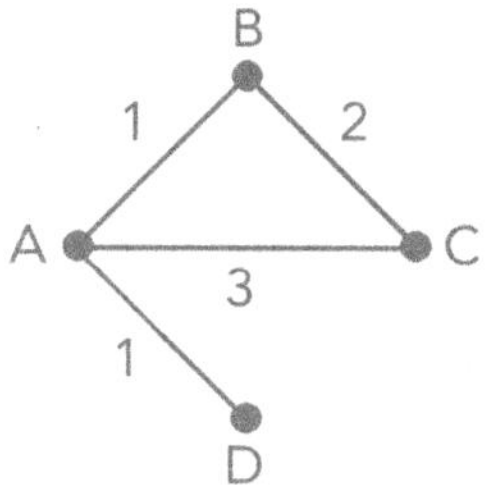

$$
\begin{array}{cccc}
A & B & C & D
\end{array}
\equiv
\begin{pmatrix}
0 & 1 & 3 & 1 \\
1 & 0 & 2 & 0 \\
3 & 2 & 0 & 0 \\
1 & 0 & 0 & 0
\end{pmatrix}
\begin{array}{c}
A \\ B \\ C \\ D
\end{array}
\tag{3}
$$

Measuring social capital in a group by synchronizing the weights of the nodes in order to enhance the predicative power of the mathematics is a viable way to refine accuracy of the metric and extract analytics. That said, because measuring intangibles is so concerning and includes so many random variables, despite the predictive power of the synchronized weighted calculation it would be hard to integrate it into group acceptance. In economics, the current stance on valuing intangibles is with the symmetry principle and the equivalence of tangible and intangible value.

Symmetry between tangible and intangible capital is less apparent, which is perhaps one reason that intangibles have traditionally not been counted as capital. Indeed, some

have argued – particularly in the accounting world – that
several characteristics of intangibles disqualify them from
being counted as capital; namely, the lack of *verifiability*
for intangible assets that are not acquired through market
transactions; the lack of *visibility* of intangible assets after their
acquisition that complicates efforts to track past vintages;
the *non-rivalness* of some intangible assets; and the lack
of *appropriability* of the returns from some intangibles.

It seems in economics that valuing the intangibles has
the same challenges as in social science. The draw of the
economic approach and mathematical explanation is that
our culture has accepted the approach into its current
belief system and paradigms. We may then have a higher
confidence in the predictive power as it has been significantly
considered and vetted by the financial industry.

 So one refined approach in economics is the fiscal multiplier
is the ratio of a change in national income to the change in
government spending that causes it. More generally, the
exogenous spending multiplier is the ratio of a change in
national income to any autonomous change in spending
(private investment spending, consumer spending, government
spending, or spending by foreigners on the country's exports)
that causes it. When this multiplier exceeds one, the enhanced
effect on national income is called the multiplier effect.
The mechanism that can give rise to a multiplier effect is
that an initial incremental amount of spending can lead to
increased consumption spending, increasing income further
and hence further increasing consumption, etc., resulting
in an overall increase in national income greater than the
initial incremental amount of spending. In other words, an
initial change in aggregate demand may cause a change
in aggregate output (and hence the aggregate income
that it generates) that is a multiple of the initial change.

We may be able to leverage this approach and underlying
math to design a social capital measurement. By investing

in activities that strengthen social ties, we could look
for the resultant revenue generation from the group
and then synchronize a weighted multiplier.

In economics, hyperbolic discounting is another accepted
mathematical tool that represents the intangible value of
time. It is a time-*inconsistent* model of discounting. The
discounted utility approach: intertemporal choices are no
different from other choices, except that some consequences
are delayed and hence must be anticipated and discounted
(i.e., reweighted to take into account the delay). Given two
similar rewards, humans show a preference for one that arrives
sooner rather than later. Humans are said to *discount* the
value of the later reward, by a factor that increases with the
length of the delay. This process is traditionally modeled in
form of exponential discounting, a time-*consistent* model
of discounting. A large number of studies have since
demonstrated that the constant discount rate assumed in
exponential discounting is systematically being violated.
[1] Hyperbolic discounting is a particular mathematical model
devised as an improvement over exponential discounting, in
the sense that it better fits the experimental data about actual
behavior. But note, the time inconsistency of this behavior has
some quite perverse consequences. Hyperbolic discounting
has been observed in both human and non-human animals.

Another location for some inspiration is networks in nature
sciences. For biology and the mathematical modeling of
biological phenomena to advance, the symmetrical and
algorithmic properties of organic shaping have been deeply
studied. These properties manifest themselves in that
the structure and behavior of the set of individual parts
in algorithmically organized biological structures that are
coordinated by finite parametrical groups (and semi-groups)
of non-Euclidean transformations, above all Mobius and affine.
Another approach to mathematically representing biological

networks is by using eigengene with high eigengene factorizability $EF(X^{(q)})$. Geometric interpretation of gene coexpression networks may have important theoretical and practical implications that may guide the development and application of network methods. While network methods are increasingly used in biology, the network vocabulary of computational biologists tends to be far more limited than that of, say, social network theorists. The geometric interpretation of gene coexpression network analysis reveals a deep connection to other statistical methods. Since it projects the gene expressions profiles onto the hypersphere in an m-dimensional Euclidean space, network analysis can be considered a special case of directional statistics. When focusing on the use of module eigengenes, network analysis can be considered a variant of oblique factor analysis.

It seems, through analysis, that the best way to emulate a social network is to focus on the "big picture" mathematical structure and not the individual variables. Research, despite the area of study, into networks all have a similar discovered mathematical pattern. Exponential, logarithmic or hyperbolic patterns are identified and subsequently justified as the best fit for the application. We have seen this same investigative pattern in the development of a math that represents human vision. An evolution from exponential to a more refined hyperbolic pattern. As such, we assume that hyperbolic geometry underlies these networks, and that it heterogeneous degree distributions and strong clustering in complex networks emerge naturally as simple reactions of the negative curvature and metric property of the underlying hyperbolic geometry. There is also a strong correlation between enhanced heterogeneity and that this efficiency is remarkably robust with respect to even catastrophic disturbances and damages to the network structure. Hyperbolic Geometry of Complex Networks Phys. Rev. E 82, 036106 (2010)

"Without philosophy we are just crashing around blindly in the dark. Nothing is more distressing than watching the current crop of bureaucrats demand that philosophy have a utility value, its an indication that the barbarians are winning." CATHERINE MCDONALD

THE DEMOCRATIC OPPORTUNITY

Too often, democracy is conceived as an eternal and fixed structure, not in need of continual improvement. This paper, on the other hand, urges and anticipates future political infrastructure developments, such as pubic practices of proxy-voting (already a staple of corporate decision-making processes). Improvements on governmental models explored in this paper seek to bolster participation and confidence of voters by improving communication practices between the government and the citizenry. Stronger communication can be achieved primarily by reducing the cultural gap between these groups. Communication models serve as a foundation for civic society. A robust organization requires a solid communication framework that liberates (rather than inhibits) communication with its members. Such frameworks consider the effect of verbal or written communication, as well as practices around timing, tone, gestures, expressions and postures. From a qualitative perspective, even silence forms a significant part of our communication stratagem or accidental effects. Improved communication allows for increases in available data, organized learning, systems thinking and feelings of belonging.

Effective governmental or business communication includes verifiable data (such as measurement). A receiver who verifies measurements contained in a message has confidence in the sender. The statement

"260 m² is the size of our new, employee kitchen," for example,
can be verified by those meant to enjoy the facility. The message
is clear and contains a verifiable quantity. By contrast, "the new,
employee kitchen is large enough for your needs" cannot be
verified (it expresses only an opinion) and a receiver will likely
have little confidence in the sender of this message, due to
the absence quantifiable data. Such messages are vague and,
therefore, subject to interpretation and distortion. In a political
or corporate context, one must consider not only the content of
a message but also the qualitative context of communications.

From Communication Set Theory, we know that information
passes through a number of filters in the minds of both sender
and receiver. The wording of communications, then, must be
thoughtful and precise. Ambiguity on the part of a sender is
a detriment to effective communication and will increase the
likelihood of a receiver making interpretative value judgments
or ignoring messages completely. The received meaning of a
message may be different from, or even opposite to, the meaning
intended by the sender. The principle of hermeneutics states
that the receiver/listener determines the meaning of a given
message, not the sender/speaker. And so, a robust organization
must monitor, review and improve its communication practices
overtime. Without the ability to analyze and shape decision-
making processes, then, organizations operate as hapless
extensions of their environments, beliefs and markets. Strong
organizations (businesses and governments alike) control not only
their decisions but their process for making decisions as well.
While decisions that address quantifiable data are repeatable,
decisions that rely on qualitative data are, in a sense, undecidable
and require more nuanced and finessed considerations.
However, flexible and nuanced decision-making frameworks
can guide difficult and intangible considerations.

When groups increase in size, they alter their environment.
Adaptability of groups depends on clear and concise
communication, while an inability to adapt could prove fatal.
Only organizations that can respond to new challenges will

survive. Autopoietic organizations (i.e., those that can adapt to their environment) retain their identity and core values amid change and possess strong "defensive" structures. One method of ensuring a flexible group structure is to install heterarchical relations between group members. Heterarchy can be defined as anti-hierarchical structure or as systems that allow group members to adopt a multiplicity of rank and function. Such systems benefit from the various potentials of individuals, at a given time. A political system that continuously adapts to its constituents and environment collects, stores, processes and disseminates information important for the organization and its members.

Improving Democratic decision-making processes can best be achieved by harvesting multiple perspectives. Although various type of analytics and metrics can provide tangible support to information, one must balance and augment data processing tools with human intuition and judgment. Organizations that do not understand the models of information gathering and analysis that they employ obtain weak data and make faulty decisions. Effective businesses and governments must understand what assumptions effect their data and decisions (such as a privileging of quantitative over qualitative data).

In the 21st century, governance and social organization form the subjects of increasingly complex debates. In countries the size of Canada, England, or even Sweden, representative governments face particular challenges for fair and equitable distribution of goods and services. Democratic governments, especially those overseeing large jurisdictions, must ensure that their perception of citizen need is not based on regional voting levels. People living in remote areas may feel unconnected from distant political centers, where leaders they will never meet are paid to represent them. Such regions often produce lower voter turn-outs than urban areas (or even more accessible rural areas) but the situations and needs of citizens in outlying regions are often the most extreme ones. Often, those communities that government hears from least that most require governmental support. Ironically, direct access to leaders often comes from financial contributions to campaigns and individuals in a position to donate monies are those whose needs are, inherently, least urgent.

Another challenge to fair governance, for any jurisdiction, is that political ideals do not always reflect political realities. Governments, even Democratically elected governments, too often exploit their positions of power and conduct themselves in a manner contrary to the system they are entrusted to uphold. Many shortcomings and loopholes complicate and degrade our current political system. One solution to political strife, currently being tested by some countries is the introduction of proxy voting systems. Proxy voting (also known as "Liquid" or "Delegative" democracy) encourages people who have already taken an interest in government to participate more fully, by leveraging existing trust relationships. These systems also leverage modern technology to ameliorate some of the flaws in our Democratic practices. By increasing ease of voting, Liquid Democracy bolsters citizen engagement in political systems. In countries such as Germany, Liquid Democracy has been the subject of experiments in the political and corporate sectors. Introducing transfers of votes into the Canadian system would require significant changes to structural voting mechanisms as well as to our established notions of ballot casting. Citizen perception of and trust in the electoral system must shift to accommodate modern solutions to voting technologies and practices. Such a shift will require the integration of communication theory into governance philosophies and practices.

The current governing systems of many large organizations encourages delegates to make important decisions based on quantitative analysis and only quantitative metrics determine electoral decisions. For example, in elections, an organization or government may simply count how many votes each candidate (or policy) receives and the first one "past the post" will win. One problem with this system is the difficulty of ascertaining which candidate can best represent voters, as a local candidate's merit becomes confused with his or her political party and the branding system that backs them. Blurring the line between party ideologies and an individual's merit makes a candidate's ethics, experience and decision-making ability very difficult to ascertain, for voters. This may be an inevitable drawback of any large system of governance but it still contributes significantly to a sense of distrust on the part of the Democratic voter. The ability to transfer votes to trusted individuals would encourage political dialogue, citizen engagement and, thereby, active voting. Proxy voting systems emphasize qualitative relationships, by passing votes onto people of shared values and trusted knowledge. Modern governments demonstrate progress and innovation in many areas. However, Democratic systems (at least in principle) encourage continual improvement and renovation. The main advantage of Democracy is that such changes to our system come from established, transparent processes and do not require violent revolutions at the cost of human lives.

Bryan Ford, originator of the concept of Delegative Democracy states that he developed the idea as a way to scale "Direct Democracy" beyond the level of small communities. His version of Delegative Democracy encourages participation, which Direct Democracy depends upon. But Ford's system does not assume unlimited time and knowledge on the part of every voter. Someone uncertain about the bevy of candidates in a given election may seek the advice of a friend, family member or colleague, who they perceive as knowledgeable and whose values they admire. Rather than have that individual merely advise a voter, Delegative Democracy would have that person act as a voting delegate for another voter. Ford writes that "participatory approaches to democracy are important because they address a fundamental security flaw in representative democracy, which in practice allows small groups of elite political insiders to control and limit voting" (Ford, 2002). Ford, then, envisions a system of democracy marked by ultimate flexibility and liberty: "voters may choose to participate in some meetings directly, overriding their delegate's choices in those meetings, and voters may revoke or change their delegation at any time" (Ford, 2002). In his article, Ford states that the idea of Liquid Democracy has circulated in a variety of forms since the 1880s, attracting the attention of many political thinkers and authors including, notably, Lewis Carrol.

The long history of vote delegation both bolsters and impedes the possibility of implementing proxy-voting beyond the corporate governance model, into civic governance. While many thinkers have contributed to and refined mainstream perspectives on Delegative Democracy, the seeming non-start of the idea may serve to delimit academic interest in a movement that is seen as obscure or as a novelty. The system's originator and ardent proponent, Bryan Ford, writes that "Delegative Democracy combines the best elements of direct and representative democracy by replacing artificially imposed representation structures with an adaptive structure founded on real personal and group trust relationships" (Ford, 2002). Liquid Democracy, then, seems compatible with the contemporary moment, in which digital technologies heighten our connectivity and ability to think and act in large groups.

Even those individuals who find themselves elected to represent jurisdictions, as professional politicians, cannot amass an adequate understanding of the myriad and complex issues which they are entrusted to oversee. For example, the U.S. House of Representatives constitutes the largest parliamentary body on the planet. With so many bills and votes before the House at any given time, each of its members can only commit to engage deliberations of one or two issues concurrently. Like citizens choosing between candidates for office, even elected representatives base many decisions on "vague impressions, party alignment" and on "quid pro-quo deals" (Ford, 2002). Delegative Democracy combines Representative and Direct Democracy, leveraging the best aspects of each system, offering voters a direct choice of representatives. For voters in a Delegative Democracy, choice of delegates is limited only by the size of a given population. By opening up the representative role to the entire population (with each member a potential delegate), Liquid Democracy seeks to disperse and decentralize power. Delegative Democracy may not be a direct solution to governmental corruption, and abuses of power, but it does give the electorate greater freedom in granting power and makes delegates directly accountable for their decisions. The privilege of acting as a delegate is not a fixed position, like the privilege of representation. Voters transfer power to a delegate, then, rather than grant them power. Delegative Democracy also promotes positive community building by reducing the competition element inherent to the representative system. In the current state of Canadian Democracy, a vote either "wins" or "loses," depending on the whim of the majority of voters in a given district or riding. In Delegative Democracy, each voter can select a representative (or vote independently) so that one's choice is not at odds with the choices of his or her neighbours. Rather, each voter's delegate carries the voices of his or her supporters forward.

Implementing Delegative Democracy comes with its own host of challenges, just as Representative Democracy faces the challenge of disenfranchised citizens and Direct Democracy faces a limitation of scale. Ford addresses a number of issues for Liquid Democracy in his paper, *Delegative Democracy* (Ford, 2002) and finds challenges to implementation formidable but not insurmountable. For example, Ford considers the question of how to manage a large population of delegates, as compared to the too small population of representatives in current parliamentary systems. Another issue, relating to the size of the delegate population, relates to remuneration. If a nation, province, city, town or rural area can financially afford to support only a small handful of representatives, how will delegates be motivated and compensated in a Delegative system? Ford's paper suggests a number of solutions to these and other problems but also emphasizes that Delegative voting structures must adapt to fit organizational and individual need (Ford, 2002). In other words, each Delegative system adopted must result from democratic debate and negotiation.

The problem of overly-large delegate groups relates to the practical need for coherent debate surrounding important issues. For example, if one million voters transfer their votes to ten-thousand delegates, it would not be practical for those delegates to gather in a single location to hold discussion and debate in the manner of traditional governments. Digital platforms, however, offer solutions to the problem of having potentially millions of delegates researching, debating and deciding on important issues and legislation. Models for such digital communication systems have been successfully developed and employed by organizations such as the German Pirate Party and the Net Party of Argentina.

In his article, Ford discusses, at some length, the process of re-delegation, whereby a large number of delegates could opt out of their active decision-making role by re-delegating the votes of their supporters onto a smaller number of delegates who possess specialized knowledge on particular issues. As for the problem of how to compensate delegates in Liquid Democracy, citizens may find that Delegates do not require salaries. Compared to what is required from career politicians in our current system, we might consider a delegate an amateur or hobbyist politician. If power incites corruption, any steps taken that remove power from our systems of governance should help clean up our democracies. However, in the minds of committed delegates, a lack of salary may also help justify abuses of power that lead to personal gain and alternative forms of compensation. One solution may be to award minor compensation to a delegate for each vote entrusted to them. However, that suggestion sets Liquid Democracy on a dangerous path toward our current system's obscene campaign-financing and possibly to vote-buying, the very problems that Liquid systems of voting are intended to combat. If the threat of corruption can prevent experiments with Liquid Democracy, however, extant corruption ought to necessitate abandoning the current Representative system. The authors of this paper hold that corruption proliferates in a vertically authoritative society and reduced in communities of lateral empowerment.

Ford states that "the low cost of entry to becoming a delegate should ensure that most delegates don't accumulate inordinate amounts of voting power, since individuals who 'follow' a delegate for a while are likely to split off, become delegates themselves and try to attract their own following if the group they are in starts to become overly fat" (Ford, 2002). While Ford's article stresses the importance of unlimited choice among delegates, for voters, it is unclear why or how the number of supporters a delegate receives should be limited. If hundreds of thousands of individuals decide to support a single delegate, limiting the size of that delegate's representatives is also a limitation on the choice of those voters. However, the goal of Delegative Democracy is to counteract the overly-centralized power that erodes the integrity of our current, representative system. Ford's article does not take up another issue for the implementation of Liquid voting: the issue of the buying and selling of votes. Critics of Liquid Democracy might envision a plutocracy developing, that allows for not only delegation of votes but the outright selling of votes. That concept will offend many supporters of Democracy, for values traditional to the marketplace are generally considered inappropriate to citizens' engagement of the political process. However, we have seen over the history of Democracy in North America that markets and governance cannot be separated. Even if a Delegative system did not allow for the legal purchase of votes, that rule would prove difficult to enforce. The mechanisms, tools and rules of vote transfers would work more efficiently in the context of encryption, privacy and a user interface designed for every demographic. Although we have established personal liberty and anonymity in regard to parliamentary votes, selling a vote would constitute a violation of our political freedom.

Challenges inherent to the structure of Delegative Democracy (discussed above), while challenging, are small in comparison to the difficult process of introducing a new system of governance. Yet, every major societal system in widespread use today comes from humble beginnings and faced, at one time, challenges of social acceptance and structural implementation. It is difficult

today to imagine the foundational challenges and growing
pains faced by our ancestors, as they sought to introduce
the first Democratic and Parliamentary systems. A fear of the
unknown is unavoidable but it must not prevent the evolution
of society. Why does risk of a new system outweigh, for many,
the known dysfunction of the present state? It is perhaps only
disengagement and apathy on the part of so many citizens
that allows the current system to stand, despite a barrage of
political scandals. Ford notes that Delegative Democracy fosters
participation of citizens in governance, in either active rolls
(becoming a delegate) or passive ones (assigning a delegate).
Assigning a delegate offers citizens a middle ground between
making an informed decision (which requires knowledge, time
and effort) and abstaining altogether from the parliamentary
process. Further, rather than electing a representative to a
fixed term of office, delegates' positions are held for as long
as they are committed to serving the parliamentary processes
and for as long as they maintain the trust of their supporters.
Because revoking support from a delegate is a much easier
process for an unsatisfied voter than removing a career
politician from his or her position, Ford writes that delegates
will be compelled to "think broadly and independently and to
represent their community even-handedly instead of catering
to the needs or demands of a specific few" (Ford, 2002).

Introducing delegative structures slowly to our current system
would give Canadians a chance to experience the benefits
and drawbacks of a new system of voting, where an overnight
and totalized shift may be too disruptive to governance.
A delegative system comes with benefits as well as risks.
Honest proponents of Liquid Democracy must consider both.
Moves toward a Delegative voting structure and improved
communication models will decrease voter apathy by promoting
active and/or passive participation in democracy. While every
member of a population, despite having the right to vote,
cannot be expected to become educated on every important

issue, electing one representative from a small group of candidates—our current system—does not entrust the voters with sufficient autonomy in decision making. Delegative Democracy promotes trust in voters, who can identify leaders in their community that represent their values and beliefs on particular legislative matters. Delegates, generally, will possess greater knowledge for specific issues than those who they represent. It is primarily a delegate's expertise which attracts voters to delegate votes to him or her. In the current system, representatives do not necessarily possess or develop specialized knowledge for issues that they oversee, as they are elected as generalists, responsible for any motion that comes to a parliamentary vote. Partly for that reason, campaign speeches contain more vague rhetoric than intricacies of public policy. While candidates need only demonstrate a greater knowledge of societal issues than their select counterparts, delegates compete for voters' trust against the entire population of potential voters and delegates. In Delegative Democracy, a voter is given the widest possible choice of delegates or may choose to retain their vote for themselves.

Delegative Democracy builds community by leveraging the power of existing trust relationships, rather than relying on voters to approve candidates who they most likely have not and will never meet in person and, therefore, do not engage with, in trust relationships. Unlike our current system, Delegative Democracy does not divide a population neatly into an electorate and their elected representatives. Rather, each individual can vote directly on an issue and allocate their voice to a trusted member of the community. A citizen who wishes to speak on behalf of their fellow citizens can gain as few or as many supporters as their trustworthiness and ambition allows. The activity of delegates, in a Liquid Democracy, can be monitored more closely than elected officials in Representative Democracies, who operate at far removes from the communities which they are entrusted to serve.

"Whom do you fear
the most?" ZAN BOAG

IMPROVING DEMOCRACY THROUGH PROXIES

The transfer of votes in a Liquid Democracy can create close communities across otherwise indomitable distances (generational, cultural or geographic). Individually selected vote digital delegations, as opposed to more familiar forms of paper elections, will generate on-line versions of neighbourliness, a feeling that is integral to the democratic principle, if not its practice. As the case study of the German Pirate Party demonstrates, the increase in participation that comes with Liquid Democratic systems relies on modern software and digital platforms. A key development to existing platforms of Liquid Democracy will be to modify the vote transfer algorithm so that it includes a value enhancing "trust" metric, capable of translating qualitative value into quantitative measurements. Further, to ensure accessibility for all citizens, a phone application for landlines as well as cell phones would be a minimum requirement for ensuring the greatest number of citizens have access to the platform. Liquid Democracy can be viewed as a type of relativistic Democracy.

On the academic front, Paolo Boldi and his associates developed *Viscous Democracy*, a transitive proxy voting algorithm based on Google's *PageRank* and in a vein similar to *Structural Deep Democracy*. Wybo Wiersma explored the integration of Delegative Democracy into social networking systems (such as

Facebook) and Yefim Leifman has explored ways to implement
transitive delegation schemes using cryptography. The topic
of cryptographic implementation is of major interest to the
company Nemalux (co-owned by the author of this paper),
since a major motivation of the Nemalux *Dissent* project was
to build practical, anonymous communication systems that
would enhance the company's internal communication and
provide secure deliberation mechanisms, such as voting.
Entrusting Nemalux employees with a decision-making role
has created a strong sense of community in the work place.
Our hope, as a company, is that more system-builders and
security/privacy researchers will be bold enough to venture
into this space: democratization in the private sector.

Perhaps the most exciting development in this nascent field
began in 2006, when free software organizations in Germany
began building two different software platforms for delegation-
based online discussion and deliberation: *LiquidFeedback* and
Adhocracy. LiquidFeedback was adopted by the *German Pirate
Party,* as recounted in an article by Björn Swierczek (Swierczek,
2011). Further information on these tools and their adoption is
now available in book form and in the electronic journal, *Liquid
Democracy Journal.* Public platforms for communication have
produced smart, secure thinking and crowd-sourced wisdom.
Such innovations will surely continue to effect public policy,
enterprise decision-making and cultural practices. At a city-wide
level, ingrown social networks (in the form of interlocking company
directorates and community clubs) have been found, by Safford,
to handle major economic crisis less effectively than diverse, open
social networks (both personal and institutional) (Safford, 2009).

Decreasing voter apathy, improving concise voter communication
and increasing civic education are necessary steps to recovering
faith in and effectiveness of governance in Canada. These
goals can be achieved by creating a representative structure
with higher resolution. Focusing on smaller groups, within the
current democratic infrastructure, would improve confidence
in government efficiency. Horizontal communication across

small and large groups is made possible by social media
and new technologies. Enabling these groups can be done
by integrating a slightly modified democratic structure.

We all know that democracy is far from perfect but its
imperfection is inevitable. There is no such thing as the "perfect
form of government" on earth, but any other form of government
produces even less desirable results than does Democracy. Public
affairs are best managed by including the voices of as many
citizens as possible. Today, the majority of Democratic countries
in the world are republics, political systems structured around
elected officials. Democracy not only the best but also, by far, the
most challenging form of government—both for politicians and for
the people. The term Democracy comes from the Greek language
and means "rule by the people." Democracy has manifested in a
number of different forms that can be grouped, in broad strokes,
into two categories: Direct Democracy and Representational
Democracy. Both categories share a concern for how the body
populous (of eligible voters) executes its will. Eligible citizens in a
Direct Democracy actively participate in governing the decision
making of the government. In Representational Democracy,
citizens primarily exercise power by selecting a small number of
citizens to make decision on behalf of the entire population.

Direct Democracy is subject to some of the same vulnerabilities
as is Representative Democracy. A common criticism of the
Democratic process, in general, is the threat of irrational voters.
Since voters are often highly uninformed about political issues,
their votes often express biases rather than wisdom. We do not
adequately educate citizens in our society and so voting decisions
too often reflect motivations of personal interest, rather than
foresight for what actions will better the community. Even voters
who pay attention to party platforms, campaigns and associated
debates may be influenced by relatively inconsequential factors
(such as the personal charisma of the candidates). Promises
of short-term financial benefit may also sway a voter in his or
decision, come election day. The right to vote is unquestioned in
our society; however, our Democratic system does not associate

duties (such as a duty to inform oneself prior to voting) with this right. While Democracy entrusts important decision making to the majority will of the populous, Canada invests very little in civic education. Some may feel that politicians take advantage of low levels of political literacy. Some politicians strategize their election campaigns along the lines of marketing, rather than within the context of ideological and policy differences. Government policies, when political marketing succeeds, are the product of non-specialist opinions and are thereby compromised. This problem becomes magnified when political issues involve technically sophisticated matters, as the percentage of voters who understand an issue will be low, in such instances. Direct Democracy creates opportunities for citizens to make meaningful contributions to decision making and seeks to broaden the range of people who have access to such opportunities. Since, in the 21st century, large amounts of information inform political decisions, computer technology supports the empowerment of citizens and encourages participatory models of citizenship. Digital tools enable and enhance community narratives and the accretion of knowledge. Questions of how to effectively increase the scale of participation and translate group activity into larger networks are, today, the focus of important sociological research. Some readers may object to an insistence on digital solutions to societal problems. A de-emphasise of the importance of face to face meetings, and an over-reliance on technology, could itself reduce social engagement, even while it bolsters communication. Some scholars argue for refocusing the term on community-based activity within the domain of civil society, based on the belief that a strong non-governmental public sphere is a precondition for the emergence of a strong liberal Democracy. These scholars tend to stress the value of separation between the realm of civil society and the formal political realm.

Recent experiments in Direct Democracy include reconstruction planning for New Orleans, in the wake of Hurricane Katrina. Thousands of ordinary citizens participated in drafting and approving municipal plans. In 2011, Participatory Democracy became a notable feature of the Occupy movement. Occupy protest camps around the world based decisions on the outcomes presented by working groups, where every member could contribute and through general assemblies which filtered, refined and planned implementations for the findings of working groups. The decision-making process employed in camps of the Occupy movement successfully combined equality and mass participation in community deliberation. These successes, however, came at a cost. These demonstrations of Direct Democracy followed a very slow pace. By November of 2011, the movement had been frequently criticized in media for not coalescing around clearly identifiable aims (although participants may have argued that the visible, global experiment in Participatory Democracy was the movement's goal). Shortly thereafter, the movement largely disbanded.

Principles of Direct Democracy include:

- Group power (individual sovereignty without authority)

- Inclusiveness

- Commitment to the Democratic process

- Democratic relationships (acknowledgment of individuality, affirmation of competence, recognition of mutuality)

- Democratic deliberation (equal and adequate opportunities to speak, listening)

Obstacles to Direct Democracy include:

- Excessive meeting lengths

- Unequal commitment to group goals

- Cliques and "mini-consensus"

- Differences in communication skills and styles

- Interpersonal conflicts (and conflicts of interest)

- Dependence on emotional decisions (rather than "big picture" logic)

Social media has created a serious disruption to methods of community building in the 21st century, although we have yet to witness the extent of its implications for Democracy. Social media sites have altered the nature of information delivery, journalism, business organization and marketing. At a severe cost to the status quo, new technological platforms and tools have profoundly energized the central nervous system of our society. Despite social networking's strong track record for generating democratic engagement, many voters remain cynical and disengaged from the political process. In the future, digital technology will have greater power to bolster and limit political influence because those tools will help citizens access and evaluate political information. One worrisome development in the contemporary period is the massive citizen disengagement from politics and feelings of alienation on the part of voters. Social media offers opportunity for leadership to re-connect citizens with their representatives, bridge the citizen-government communication divide and improve public responsiveness and accountability. With the help of social media, ordinary citizens can become agents of persuasion and leverage their personal network in support of an endless variety values, issue positions or ideological stances. Today, Smart phones enable activists to reach entirely new audiences and involve them in the political process. By enabling access to information, digital technology accelerates news cycles and places a premium on electronic resources.

While every successful company places a value on the feedback of its customers, it can be difficult to compile an exhaustive list of relevant stakeholders. For almost all product development projects, more than one group of people must be considered (although the degree of relevance will vary across groups). For example, stakeholders in the development of a bedside heart monitor used in hospitals would include the various groups within the company producing the product (e.g., manufacturing, design, shipping, purchasing), the administrators within the hospital who are concerned with how much the goods cost, doctors and nurses who deploy the device, patients who will be hooked up to it and service people who will have to perform maintenance and repairs. And even this list is incomplete. Thoughtful companies will assign each stake holder's voice a unique weight (which not to say equal weight). Thoughtful compromise will resolve conflicting needs across groups. Considering the needs of all stakeholders can be seen as wise, profit-driven business practice but it can also be seen as an extension of Democratic beliefs.

To summarize: of the many ways to govern society which have been tried throughout human history, the Democratic approach, despite its flaws, has been the most successful. Democracy is particularly well suited to modern societies, with their associated rapid rate of change (Slater and Bennis, 1990). We must, however, continue to improve systems of governance for the benefit of all citizens. Current efforts to create advanced communication and voting tools result in hardware advances and community sharing software programs. In the information age, people can access knowledge like never before. As a result, many citizens access (or desire) information that can improve the quality of their lives. Access to information demands greater transparency from figures of authority, delimiting the opportunity for corruption. Opaqueness has been a hallmark of both business and government transactions in Canada, since the founding of the nation—from the building the national railroad to current construction bidding processes, to the oil tariff regime in Alberta. A long and irritating history justifies suspicion of government, on the part of the electorate. It is therefore in the best interests of any institution connected to government to avoid the external appearance of bias and, internally, mitigate bias through inclusion, intelligence and compassion. Involving the public in decision making directly, operating through transparent processes and prioritizing public auditing all promote a culture of trust and engagement.

Today, corruption threatens to undermine trust in corporations, just as it has significantly eroded the integrity of public institutions. Any organization run by human beings contains vulnerabilities. The less responsible a system appears, the more people will attempt to exploit those weaknesses. Drafting and publicizing plans for responding to crises will not suffice. Corporations, like governments, must implement preventative measures—for the sake of their survival and the good of the society which supports them. Involving the greatest possible number of stake holders (citizens or employees) in decision making strengthens the network of support. Centralizing power, on the other hand, threatens security by weakening trust and belonging. Governments and business executives can contribute positively to society by limiting waste and error and demonstrating a commitment to responsiveness, respect and inclusiveness. Inclusiveness, here, indicates not only an understanding of the value of many kinds of people but also many kinds of information (e.g., qualitative as well as quantitative). Delivering clear messages, goals and reasoning for decisions promotes trust which leads to greater engagement, at the workplace or in the public arena.

Wholly Owned Subsidiaries (WOS) form the locus of entitlement, opacity and corruption in the public arena. Through a mandate of promoting and serving Canada and Canadians, governments may install Crown Corporations, for the benefit of the nation. Through WOSs, federal, provincial and municipal services can migrate into the private sector, while maintaining a link to government funding. The efficiencies and flexibility of Crown Corporations hold strong attraction in our current socio-economic environment, as they combine public policy and commercial interests. They advance governmental policies, priorities and objectives (essential goods and services; fostering economic development; regulating sensitive or risky industries; and community and nation building). Any number of relevant and practical reasons justify establishing entities that operate at an arms'-length from the parent governmental body. These include financial security and speed of change. However, Crown Corporations involve lower levels of accountability than are usually associated with public institutions.

What purpose and mandate necessitates the need for governmental corporations (such as Canada Post or the CBC)? Transport Authorities and land development companies (for example) possess many advantages over bureaucratic oversight. These include:

X Eschewing the legislated regulations and policies which prevent a governing body from conducting certain activities directly.

X Hiring specialized talent to undertake work which public budgets could not otherwise afford. (Limited public salaries cannot realistically compete in certain markets).

X Speed of service. Bureaucracies are notoriously slow in accomplishing results, whereas the private sector excels in innovative and nimble execution of tasks.

X Independently formed polices and structures, customized to highly specified activities (which are not always properly balanced with appropriate checks and balances).

X Forming a WHS can limit liabilities and therefore promote levels of risk-taking common to the private sector but not feasible within the public realm (where financial loss can end political careers).

Creating a wholly owned subsidiary is a significant legal and administrative process which, by definition, reduces the direct control of a government (municipal, provincial or federal) over delivery of services. A clear case for the necessity of independence ought to be developed, prior to launching a WHS. Clear statements of purpose go beyond articulating underlying immediate business goals; they require comprehensive information about why private entities better serve those business purposes and wider community needs. However, such discussions often do not include the public. Currently, the fundamental reason to create a WOS is to operate outside of the current government infrastructure and outside established public policy. Public policies guide governmental actions, taken by the administrative and executive branches of the government.

The number of arm's-length, governmental organizations which operate outside public policy are unverified (particularly at the local levels of government) but "some basic research indicates that there are 47 federal Crown corporations and about 181 provincial Crown corporations. The provincial Crown Corporation sector contributed more than $43 billion to Canadian GDP in 2010, about 2.7 per cent of GDP, versus the federal contribution of roughly $11.8 billion, or 0.7 per cent of GDP. These statistics are generally regarded as approximations as there is very little research documenting the size of the government owned enterprise sector in Canada. In recent years, Crown Corporations have created an increasingly significant number of jobs for Canadians"

Canada contains a great number of municipalities which use a staggering variety of terms used to denote Crown Corporations (within the same province and even within the same municipality). Most large municipalities support over 25 business units that benefit from increased efficiency while furthering public policy. For example, municipal transit systems are typically large, underfunded stand-alone business units. Provincially, more room remains for potential privatization and a greater departure from public policy. By law, city councils cannot abdicate or delegate responsibility and accountability to the citizens of their municipality for the stewardship of municipal assets and funds. This basic difference between public and private organizations creates the need for a measured approach to the theoretical governance of the corporate sector. Therefore, the current culture of Crown Corporations contains dangerous potential for incubating corruption.

Some potential refinements to increase effective constituent communication and adherence of public policy to the structure of the WSO are:

- A need for accountability and transparency in governance, so that citizens can be assured their municipal assets are well managed (financially and ethically). "Together, transparency and accountability build trust. No institution, no matter its size or mandate, can remain viable for very long if the bonds of trust are broken by the failure or perceived unwillingness to disclose information, explain decisions, and justify actions. Indeed, transparency is what makes accountability possible"

X Greater consistency in the regulation of WOSs while avoiding uniformity (which would work against unique needs of the different communities and services). Any governance system must have the flexibility to adapt and adjust to the evolving needs of the populous it serves. Concurrently, leadership should develop consistent frameworks that participants can understand. The design of corporate governance bodies can be modified by the CEO, offering organizations flexibility in codes of conduct and internal structure.

X Structural frameworks must support accountability to established public policy and not degrade accountability or transparency. "There is a need to reassert the role of Crown corporations as instruments of public policy"

At present, the wholly owned subsidiaries of the City of Calgary include: the Calgary Arts Development Corporation (CADA), Attainable Homes Calgary Corporation, the Calgary Housing Company (CHC), Calgary Economic Development (CED), the Calgary Municipal Land Corporation (CMLC), ENMAX and the Calgary Parking Authority (CPA). Crown Corporations operating in the current, relaxed legislative environment create fertile soil for the possible manipulation of established democratic policies and principles. These bodies proliferate, however, because governments feel that the potential risk for increased corruption throughout these organization is balanced by the measured, financial benefit to the municipality, province or country.

Corporate Dictatorships are more agile than public Democracies, for better or worse. Democratic government, because of its participatory nature, requires greater investments of time and resources to act or evolve. However, when Democratic processes involve large numbers of decision makers, the results of those decisions will be of higher quality than those produced by sole or small executives. Business leaders—in managerial style, treatment of employees, approach to criticism and communication—can choose to model themselves after Democratic or Totalitarian heads of state. Historically, CEOs have followed the latter model (to the detriment of their companies) and hierarchical corporate structures have followed the structures of military command (Slater and Bennis, 1990). Militaries commit themselves to efficiency and enforced obedience, an ethos fit for its specific tasks. The rigidity and coercion of military culture is at odds with a Democratic vision for civic life, however. The leadership of private companies ought to ask which model of governance creates a more human and humane working environment for employees: Authoritarian or Participatory.

Public trust in the private sector is currently threatened by a perceived (and sometimes actual) prioritizing of financial performance over ethical leadership. These two central priorities need not be mutually exclusive, however. Employees, constituents and stakeholders must create an environment that inspires trust, pride and optimism. Jim Whitehurst, the CEO of Red Hat, is an influential champion of Democratic thinking within business organizations. In his book *The Open Organization*, Whitehurst puts forth a compelling argument that advocates for Democratically run corporations and specifically, the idea of meritocracy. Whitehurst believes that strong ideas are equally likely to come from an intern as from the CEO, so every single person in a corporation should have an equal say.

Organizations, like living systems, evolve and adapt in order to survive. The similarity between organizations and living systems was noted by the scientist Miroslav Baca, who borrowed the term "autopoietic" from biology. This term was first introduced into biology in 1972, by Chilean biologists Humberto Maturana and Francisco Varela. Maturana and Varela defined the self-maintaining chemistry of living cells as autopoiesis: "the property of a system which is capable of reproducing and maintaining itself" More recently, the concept has been applied to the fields of systems theory and sociology. In his 2007 paper "Autopoietic Information Systems in Modern Organizations," Baca applied the concept to information systems within organizations (Baca, 2007). In this paper, Baca writes that, "we can conclude that only organizations that can respond to these challenges will survive" and that "organisms have the ability to adapt to their environment, while being able to keep their own identity within that environment"

Open source project management systems like source forge, Ruby Forge, Libresource or Visone have evolved to facilitate the evolution of corporations in a Democratic direction. Social systems use communications as their particular mode of autopoietic reproduction. Democratic communications are recursively produced and reproduced by a network of communications which cannot exist outside of such a network (Luhmann 1986:174). Every communication refers to the fact that all participants (composers and receivers) perceive each other as present within the exchange. However, not everyone who is physically or mentally present will also be treated as present by the communication. For example, people at other tables in a restaurant, although physically present, might not be considered present by the interactional communication. British Mathematician (and originator of the Laws of Forms) Spenser Brown suggests treating observation as the most basic concept of any analysis. As a concept, it is supposed to be even more basic than e.g. that of thing, event, thought, action or communication.

Science has but one subject and only one fundamental method. Its subject matter is the array of interconnected and interacting systems we find in the universe around us, including, of course, the various social, psychological, and biological systems of primary concern to psychologists. (Joel Michell)

Challenges to Implementation

Proxy voting systems require highly finessed software functionality and privacy protection. Advanced cryptographic technology can adjust for and adapt to privacy issues and privacy legislation. Successful vote transfers depend on the trust and security of all users. The process of registration for voters, delegates, managers, or MLAs must be simple and transparent. Graphic User Interfaces (GUIs) must be intuitive, to ensure the platforms themselves do not become barriers to participation. Software and programming requirements are:

- The ability to change votes before making a final decision

- Delegate registration

- Simplicity

- Confidentiality

The above requirements create software and technology related challenges as well as human challenges. Citizens, and especially their systems, tend to be resistant to change. Fear of change, for some, could create another significant barrier to the implementation of Liquid Democracy. As a potential future state for nations around the world, Liquid Democracy must present simple, reliable tools, such as the German Pirate Party's liquid feedback platform. At present, the largest barriers (other than software and programming requirements) to implementing vote transfer systems remain accessibility, user confidence and understanding of the technologies involved.

Individuals with advanced education and income are more likely to use internet voting than those with lower levels of education and income. However, even individuals who use computers daily may not, initially, feel comfortable re-assigning vital democratic processes to computer tasks. Often, "ethnicity, income, age and education [are] significant predictors of access to technology" (Belanger & Carter, 2010). Mossenburg, Tolbert and Stansbury indicate two limitations to total computer fluency: technical competence and information literacy (Mossenburg, C, & Stansbury, 2003). Technical competence is the ability to use computer hardware (e.g., mouse, monitor and keyboard). Information literacy is the "the ability to recognize when information can solve a problem or fill a need and to effectively employ information resources" (Belanger & Carter, 2010). The requirement of these two types of literacy present significant hurdles for the implementation of Delegative Democracy because, by its very nature, Democracy must be available to all citizens. Low income, elderly or immigrant groups, as well as those with low levels of education, are vulnerable within government systems. Governments need not only ensure not that these groups can access platforms for Liquid Democracy but, further, actively encourage their participation.

Society builds organizational and institutional structures because of their reliability and functionality. On the whole, however, such structures prove resistant to change. In the short term, fixity can be viewed as a strength but can become a disability over the long term, if necessary reforms are not enacted. While institutions are designed to handle large populations, institutional structures do not readily take into account the great diversity of human conditions, aspirations and needs. (I.e., each individual in a system is treated as identical). When social institutions resist needed reform, they cause pain for the citizens they would serve. At the same time, reform itself can become a source of pain. Adequate theorizing and planning for institutional measures can reduce the difficulty of transition to new systems like Liquid Democracy. While proponents of Delegative voting work to remove barriers to Democratic developments, work is also required to design new voting structures.

Any changes to our current voting system will inevitably come with new challenges. Privacy is an increasingly important issue to citizens and constitutes the most recent addition to governmental jurisdiction in Canada. As of 2010, each province and territory has an office similar to the national office of the Federal Privacy Commissioner. Privacy violations are currently gaining increased media attention, such as the targeted hacker attacks on Sony, eBay and the American Military. However, cryptographic technologies are certainly capable of making voting with computer technologies as safe as (or safer than) traditional, paper elections. Processes of vote-switching have been well tested in the corporate and non-profit sectors and governments can leverage that learning when implementing processes for naming delegates. Because the objective of liquid democracy is to encourage greater participation in the political process, the process must not become yet another hindrance to participation.

Network engineers must work hard to program smooth, intuitive communication systems for voting. Such systems must limit information loss and interference. It is essential that such systems do not rely on a single, centralized server, which could be controlled by a small group of individuals looking to corrupt the system for their own agenda. Like Delegative voting structures, the de-centralization of power is another key to Democratic security. Although great strides have been made (such as democracyOS in Argentina), no current program can serve as a complete model for registering delegates, switching votes and maintaining the privacy of citizens. These issues must be tested, implemented and improved before Delegative Democracy can become the next step in the evolution of governmental systems, globally. Shifting the structure of government requires an adjustment to established conceptions of what role of government should play in society. Citizens resistant to change may experience greater risk in a new system than within the existing one. Those who have vested interest in the current system will likely resist any structural changes to government and protest improvements, by drawing attention to unknown factors and uncertain outcomes. The private sector, home to technological innovations, drive structural change. The public sector can learn much from the business world about how to instigate and adapt to such change.

Delegative Democracy is also vulnerable to individual bigotries. Vulnerable members of our society, those with limited access to information and financial resources, may choose not to proxy their votes on contentious issues, or may choose tabloid style populist candidates (the popularity of Donald Trump serves as a contemporary example). Novelty figures like Trump only become dangerous when large numbers of citizens throw their collective weight behind rationally indefensible positions. Unfortunately, no Democratic safe-guards protect the people from themselves. We can create no system, then, that will be entirely incorruptible. Even delegates would not always be immune to lobbyists dispensing kickbacks. However, the instinct to protect reputation and community standing would be the saving grace needed to minimize the potential impact of corrupted delegates. Ideally, problems of this nature would be short-lived and produce extremely high costs for proxies who violate public trust. We may not wish to return to the days of Athens, where citizens vowed to kill anyone who compromised Democracy; neither, however, can we continue with the current system, when guilty politicians have legal expenses covered by public monies. A Liquid Democracy pilot project is needed to test the reliability and weaknesses of the system. Refinements to a new system must come from experience as well as from consulting the population as a whole.

Delegation is just one of many improvements needed to address scaling and security issues with traditional Democratic processes. Extant tools for Delegative Democracy do not contain adequate security protections, because many depend on a single centralized server and no cryptographic protections ensure the integrity of the deliberation process. System builders must earn voter trust by making privacy, anonymity and coercion-resistance central to software designs. Delegative Democracy requires secure, scalable deliberative processes and also secure and scalable implementation of those processes (emphasizing strong, decentralized integrity and privacy protections). Building integrity-protected, privacy- and anonymity-preserving technical infrastructure and communication systems has been one of the key goals of the Nemalux group's Dissent project for the past several years.

"You can do what I cannot do. I can do what you cannot do. Together we can do great things." MOTHER TERESA

CONCLUSION

S ince its inception, democracy has provided challenges for philosophers, politicians and citizens alike. Although resolving these challenges requires intensive resources and large amounts of time, the efforts required to meet them are well worth the struggle. Only Democratic governments offer the possibility of direct citizen participation. The failures of modern Democracies are often linked directly to contemporary voting systems, voter apathy and populations challenges (distances and diversity). A potential solution to these difficulties is to create voting systems that promote the engagement of citizens in their own governance. Proxy voting encourages participation, decreases voter apathy and integrates various and marginalized voices into important debates. When successfully implemented, Liquid Democratic platforms employ flexible communication systems to transmit information between representatives and their constituents.

Democratic representation of multiple points of view, then, would predict the popularity and effectiveness of politicians in a Delegative Democracy. Representing all opinions operating within a population necessitates increasing the number of representatives or candidates. As with any innovation, we now face crucial questions and concerns about the computerization of voting and governance. However, the current system seems to face worse problems: widespread apathy, corruption and dysfunction. The chief benefit of Delegative or Liquid Democratic systems is that voters can develop quality relationships with their delegates and, thereby, increase the qualitative value of government in their lives. Direct relationships with delegates will improve the population's view of Democracy and increase trust in our political leadership. Democratic societies, as they exist today, typically deal with overly large numbers of people and, as a result, focus on quantitative over qualitative values. Liquid Democratic systems focus, instead, on evolving representation, in order to emphasize quality relationships over the number of relationships in a system. There is no limit to the improvements that could be made to our systems of governance, if we shift decision making from the few to the many.

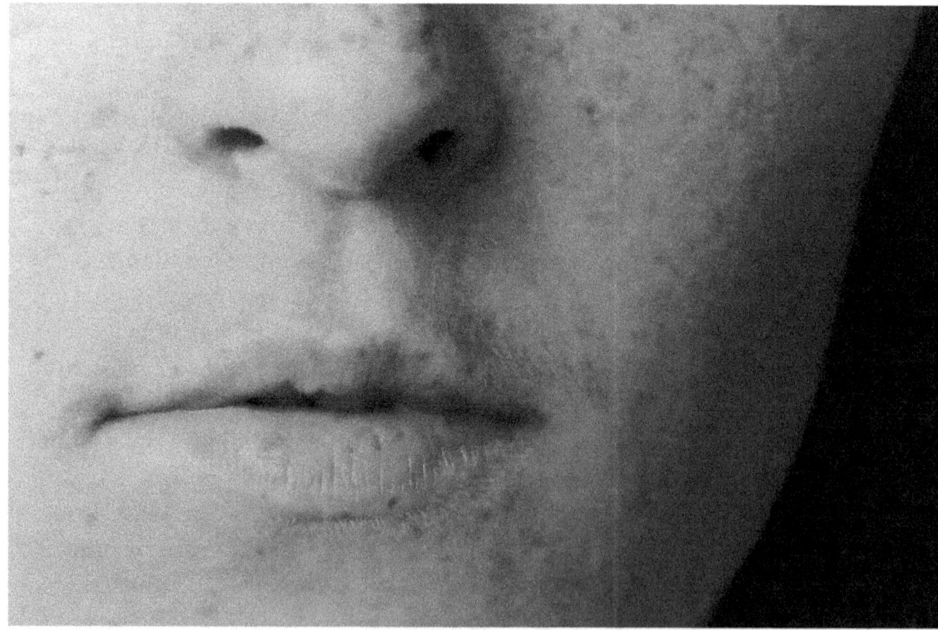

REFERENCES

Belanger, F., & Carter, L. (2010). The Impacts of the Digital Divide on Citizens' Intentions to Use Internet Voting. *International Journal on Advances in Internet Technology*, 203.

Branson, R. (n.d.). *The Biography Channel*. Retrieved from The Biography Channel Web Site: http://www.thebiographychannel.co.uk/biographies/richard-branson/quotes.html;jsessionid=566B-4B36A0FF53F22A400F83B5F3311E

Buffett, W. (1983, March 14). Chairman's Letter 1983.

Caron, B. (2012, April 23). *Cyber Social Structure*. Retrieved from A Cyber Social Structure Web Site: http://cybersocialstructure.org/2012/04/23/building-a-double-loop-for-liquid-innovation/

Cattell, J. (n.d.). *Classics in the History of Psychology*. Retrieved from A Classics in the History of Psychology Web site: http://psychclassics.yorku.ca/Cattell/mental.htm

Churchill, W. (2003, May 9). *DEMOCRACY: Democracy and Churchill*. (R. Hilton, Editor) Retrieved March 06, 2015, from A Stanford Web site: http://wais.stanford.edu/Democracy/democracy_DemocracyAndChurchill(090503).html

Ford, B. (2002). *Brynosaurus*. Retrieved from A Brynosaurus Web Site.

Ford, B. (2014, November 16). *Delegative Democracy Revisited*. Retrieved from A Bford Github Web site: http://bford.github.io/2014/11/16/deleg.html

Galton, F. (n.d.). *Life of Francis Galton by Karl Pearson*. Retrieved from A Life of Franics Galton by Karl Pearson Web site: http://galton.org/cgi-bin/searchImages/search/pearson/vol2/pages/vol2_0393.htm

Gregorius, J. (2013, December 03). *Social 3.0 Mastering the Global Transition on Our Way to Society 3.0*. Retrieved from Social 3.0 Mastering the Global Transition on Our Way to Society 3.0 Web site: http://www.society30.com/liquid-democracy-future-democracy-digital-age-2/

Meyer, D. (2012, May 7). *Techpresident*. Retrieved from A Techpresident Web site: http://techpresident.com/news/wegov/22154/how-german-pirate-partys-liquid-democracy-works

Michell, J. (2009). *Methodological Thinking in Psychology: 60 Years Gone Astray?* United States of America: Information Age Publishing.

Mossenburg, K., C, T., & Stansbury, M. (2003). *Virtual Inequality: Beyond the Digital Divide*. Washington D.C.: George Washington University Press.

Purves, D., Cabeza, R., Huettel, S. A., LaBar, K. S., Platt, M. L., & Woldorff, M. G. (2013). *Principles of Cognitive Neuroscience*. Sinauer Associates Inc.

Bača, Miroslav, Markus Schatten, and Dinko Deranja. "Autopoietic Information

Systems in Modern Organizations." *Organizacija, letnik* 40:2 (2007): 157-165. Print.

Brin, Sergey, and Lawrence Page. "The Anatomy of a Large-Scale Hypertextual Web

Search Engine." World-Wide Web Conference. Brisbane, Australia. 14 Apr. 1998. Address.

Crisan, Daria and McKenzie, Kenneth J., Government-Owned Enterprises in Canada (February

21, 2013). SPP Research Paper No. 6-8.

Friesen, Milton. "Is Social Capital Measurement Still Relevant? A Roundtable Policy

and Social Impact Assessment White Paper." *Cardus.* 2014. 8 Jul. 2015 *<https://www.cardus.ca/ store/4191/>*

Green-Armytage, James. "Direct Voting and Proxy Voting." *Constitutional Political*

Economy Jun. 2015: 190-220. Print.

Gunzelmann, Glenn. "Unified Theories of Cognition: Newell's Vision After 25 Years."

International Conference on Cognitive Modelling. Groningen, The Netherlands. 11 Apr. 2015. Address.

Iacobucci, Edward and Trebilcock, Michael J. "The Role of Crown Corporations in the

Canadian Economy: An Analytical Framework." (March 26, 2012). SPP Research Paper No. 12-9.

Michell, Joel. "The Quantity/ Quality Interchange: A Blindspot On The Highway Of

Science." *Methodological Thinking in Psychology: 60 Years Gone Astray?* Ed. Aaro Toomela and Jaan Valsiner. Charlotte: Information Age Publishing, 2010. 45-68. Print.

Michell, Joel. "History and Philosophy of Measurement: A Realist View." IMEKO TC7

International Symposium. Saint-Petersburg, Russia. 2 Jul. 2004. Address.

Siegler, Veronique. Measuring Social Capital. Measuring National Well-Being

Programme, 18 July 2014. Web. 8 July 2015.

van der Gaag, Martin. *Measurement of Individual Social Capital.* Amsterdam: F&N

Boekservices, 2005. Print.

van Zyl, Casper and Nicola Taylor. "Work Personality Index and Emotional Quotient

Inventory." *Psychometrics.* 2010. 8 Jul. 2015 <http://www. psychometrics.com/docs/wpi- eqi.pdf>

"Flat, Flexible, and Forward-Thinking: Public Service Next." *Canada's Public Policy*

Forum. 2014. 8 Jul. 2015. <http:// ppforum.ca/sites/default/files/ Flat%20Forward%20Flexible%20 Final%20Report_0.pdf>

Canada. The Federal Public Service. *Blueprint 2020: Getting Started – Getting Your Views,*

Building Tomorrow's Public Service Together. N.p.: n.p., n.d. Print.

[AS1] History and Philosophy of measurement: A Realist View (Joel Michell)

[AS2] Yi, S. K. M., Steyvers, M., Lee, M. D. and Dry, M. J. (April 2012). "The Wisdom of the Crowd in Combinatorial Problems". Cognitive Science 36 (3). doi:10.1111/j.1551-6709.2011.01223.x.

"How Social Influence can Undermine the Wisdom of Crowd Effect". Proc. Nat. Acad. Sciences, 2011.

Working With "Delegative Democracy" By Brian Ford (Http://Www.brynosaurus.com/Deleg/Deleg.pdf) À Intro To Sd2: Structural Deep Democracy***S

http://www.policyschool.ucalgary.ca/sites/default/files/research/government-owned-enterprises-final.pdf

Todorov, A. "Inferences of Competence from Faces Predict Election Outcomes." *Science* 308.5728 (2005): 1623-626. Web.

Kahnemen, Daniel. *Thinking Fast and Slow.* Anchor Canada. Print.

Ambady, Nalini. "The Perils of Pondering: Intuition and Thin Slice Judgments." *Psychological Inquiry* 21.4 (2010): 271-78. Web

Dietvorst, Berkeley J., Joseph P. Simmons, and Cade Massey.

"Algorithm Aversion: People Erroneously Avoid Algorithms after Seeing Them Err." *Journal of Experimental Psychology: General* 144.1 (2015): 114-26. Web.

Nanos White Paper: Trust in Government

Dunbar, Robin. "Coevolution of neocortical size, group size and

language in humans." *Behavioral and Brain Sciences* 16.4 (1993):   681–735

Mosaic White Paper: Communication Theory

Bryan Ford – Delegative Democracy Paper – May 15, 2002

Ford, Bryan. "Delegative Democracy Revisited." N.p., n.d. Web. 14 July 2015. http://bford.github.io/2014/11/16/deleg.html

GLOSSARY
Decision Making Biases

Name	Description
Ambiguity effect	The tendency to avoid options for which missing information makes the probability seem "unknown".
Anchoring or focalism	The tendency to rely too heavily, or "anchor", on one trait or piece of information when making decisions (usually the first piece of information that we acquire on that subject)
Attentional bias	The tendency of our perception to be affected by our recurring thoughts.
Automation bias	The tendency to excessively depend on automated systems which can lead to erroneous automated information overriding correct decisions.
Curse of knowledge	When better-informed people find it extremely difficult to think about problems from the perspective of lesser-informed people.
Decoy effect	Preferences for either option A or B changes in favor of option B when option C is presented, which is similar to option B but in no way better.
Focusing effect	The tendency to place too much importance on one aspect of an event.
Framing effect	Drawing different conclusions from the same information, depending on how that information is presented.
Hyperbolic discounting	Discounting is the tendency for people to have a stronger preference for more immediate payoffs relative to later payoffs. Hyperbolic discounting leads to choices that are inconsistent over time – people make choices today that their future selves would prefer not to have made, despite using the same reasoning. Also known as current moment bias, present-bias, and related to Dynamic inconsistency.
Rhyme as reason effect	Rhyming statements are perceived as more truthful. A famous example being used in the O.J Simpson trial with the defense's use of the phrase "If the gloves don't fit, then you must acquit."

Name	Description
Risk compensation / Peltzman effect	The tendency to take greater risks when perceived safety increases.
Selective perception	The tendency for expectations to affect perception.
Semmelweis reflex	The tendency to reject new evidence that contradicts a paradigm.
Social comparison bias	The tendency, when making hiring decisions, to favour potential candidates who don't compete with one's own particular strengths.
Social desirability bias	The tendency to over-report socially desirable characteristics or behaviours in one self and under-report socially undesirable characteristics or behaviours.
Status quo bias	The tendency to like things to stay relatively the same (see also loss aversion, endowment effect, and system justification).
Stereotyping	Expecting a member of a group to have certain characteristics without having actual information about that individual.
Subadditivity effect	The tendency to judge probability of the whole to be less than the probabilities of the parts.
Subjective validation	Perception that something is true if a subject's belief demands it to be true. Also assigns perceived connections between coincidences.
Survivorship bias	Concentrating on the people or things that "survived" some process and inadvertently overlooking those that didn't because of their lack of visibility.

Name	Description
Time-saving bias	Underestimations of the time that could be saved (or lost) when increasing (or decreasing) from a relatively low speed and overestimations of the time that could be saved (or lost) when increasing (or decreasing) from a relatively high speed.
Unit bias	The tendency to want to finish a given unit of a task or an item. Strong effects on the consumption of food in particular.[70]
Well travelled road effect	Underestimation of the duration taken to traverse oft-traveled routes and overestimation of the duration taken to traverse less familiar routes.
Zero-risk bias	Preference for reducing a small risk to zero over a greater reduction in a larger risk.
Zero-sum heuristic	Intuitively judging a situation to be zero-sum (i.e., that gains and losses are correlated). Derives from the zero-sum game in game theory, where wins and losses sum to zero. The frequency with which this bias occurs may be related to the social dominance orientation personality factor.

Social biases

Most of these biases are labeled as attributional biases.

Name	Description
Illusion of transparency	People overestimate others' ability to know them, and they also overestimate their ability to know others.

Memory Errors and Biases

Main article: List of memory biases

In psychology *and* cognitive science, a memory bias is a cognitive bias that either enhances or impairs the recall of a memory (either the chances that the memory will be recalled at all, or the amount of time it takes for it to be recalled, or both), or that alters the content of a reported memory. There are many types of memory bias, including:

Name	Description
Bizarreness effect	Bizarre material is better remembered than common material.
Choice-supportive bias	In a self-justifying manner retroactively ascribing one's choices to be more informed than they were when they were made.
Change bias	After an investment of effort in producing change, remembering one's past performance as more difficult than it actually was
Conservatism or Regressive bias	Tendency to remember high values and high likelihoods/probabilities/frequencies as lower than they actually were and low ones as higher than they actually were. Based on the evidence, memories are not extreme enough
Cross-race effect	The tendency for people of one race to have difficulty identifying members of a race other than their own.
Zeigarnik effect	That uncompleted or interrupted tasks are remembered better than completed ones.

SUPPORTING ESSAYS

"To vastly improve your country and truly make it great again, start by choosing a better leader. Do not let the media or the establishment make you pick from the people they choose, but instead choose from these they do not pick." SUZY KASSEM

A paper submitted to the Nemalux
Democracy Project on April 28, 2016.

Brief Introduction

One of the tools available to the three orders of government
in Canada is crown corporations. Their establishment has
both alleviated and created headaches for governments.
Despite an ideological assault on crown corporations
since the early 1990s, their ongoing presence is not likely
to be challenged in a serious way. Nonetheless, there
are those who seek to make them more democratically
accountable and more relevant to the times. This paper
asserts that delegative democracy can help realize these
objectives by augmenting current governance structures.

This study begins with an examination of Canadian crown
corporations in a historical context. Their origins and
initial impetus are exculpated, revealing a pattern for their
establishment. The middle section of the paper is concerned
with their processes, governance, and catalogues some of
the history of political corruption that in part defined them.
The last portion of this exposition aims to suggest a role for
delegative democracy, or proxy voting through an invention
entitled the Canadian Assembly: its potential relationship
with Canadian representative democracy and how, in
broad strokes, it may interact with crown corporations.

Impetus for Crown Corporations in Canada

The emergence of crown corporations arose through a variety of exigencies and imperatives. Most often, their creation has emanated from a series of political problems brought on by pressures (social, economic, political) that forces political entities to act. The simple definition of a crown corporation is that it is an "institution with corporate form brought into existence by action of the Government of Canada to serve a public function."[1] Crown corporations are created by all three orders of government in Canada and their orientation reflects the federated nature of the country's political system. Their creation also has a prescribed legal framework through which governments must adhere.[2]

In the Canadian context, crown corporations have become a mainstay of the institutional universe and their place are seldom questioned or given to widespread examination. The Canadian Broadcasting Corporation (CBC), for example, is now considered the centerpiece to the country's broadcasting system,[3] although federal governments have largely eviscerated it through persistent funding cutbacks. There can be little doubt that its initial emergence can be traced to a two-pronged sense of urgency on the part of the national government. Firstly, there was an inherent desire to beat back what was perceived as American cultural dominance in the day-to-day lives of the then relatively new country. Secondly, private enterprise largely eschewed grand projects that did not feature the prospect of an immediate financial return.[4]

Far from an ancillary or side issue, cultural expression in Canada seemed to lack a unifying institutional medium that could join citizens from one end of the country to the other. Canadian radio,

---

1   C.A. Ashley and Reginald George Hampden Snails, *Canadian Crown Corporations: Some Aspects of Their Administration and Control* (Toronto: Macmillan and Company, 1965). Pg. 3.

2   J. Robert S. Prichard, Crown Corporations in Canada: The Calculus of Instrument Choice (Toronto: Butterworths, 1983). Pgs. 16 & 17.

3   Marc Raboy, "The Role of Public Consultation in Shaping the Canadian Broadcasting System," Canadian Journal of Political Science 28, 3 (1995), pgs. 464 & 465.

4   Margaret Prang, "The Origins of Public Broadcasting in Canada," Canadian Historical *Review* 46, 1 (1965), pgs. 1-3.

the emerging tool that entertained vast numbers of people, was dominated by American private broadcasters who cared little to nothing for Canadian culture. Given a choice between vesting trust in U.S. broadcasters who had practiced ambivalence to Canada, and the national government, MPs chose the latter as the body that would best shape Canadian broadcasting.[5] Long, long before New Public Management thinking had enveloped government institutions,[6] it was the external threat or imperative that drove the creation of some crown institutions such as the CBC. The fear that Canadian private interests would become owned and subservient to American syndicates[7] was a decisive impetus towards Canada gravitating to the BBC (British Broadcasting Corporation) model. In this sense, the American threat was coupled and integrated with the inability of Canadian private enterprise to fill the need in question.

Accordingly, it was no surprise when the Canadian government founded the Canadian Radio Broadcasting Commission in 1932, which became the CBC in 1936. The publicly-stated reasons by Prime Minister Bennett encapsulated the belief that government was better equipped than private enterprise to fulfill the role and that Canada's national sovereignty was at stake.[8]

Government intervention had characterized the building of the Canadian Pacific Railway (CPR), namely because private enterprise assessed the risks of the project as higher than their potential bottom line profit margins.[9] Similar to the formation of the CBC, the federal government employed a type of "defensive expansionism."[10] Whereas the King and Bennett

---

5   Canada, House of Commons, Debates, May 31, 1928, pg. 3623.

6   Christopher Hood, "The 'New Public Management' in the 1980s: Variations on a Theme," Accounting, Organization and Society, 20, 2/3 (1995), pg. 94.

7   Plaunt Papers, E.H. Blake to Spry, March 13, 1931.

8   Anthony E. Boardman and Aidan R. Vining, "Public Service Broadcasting in Canada," The Journal of Media Economics 9, 1 (1996), pg. 48.

9   J.C. Herbert Emery and Kenneth J. McKenzie, "Damned if you do, damned if you don't: an option value approach to evaluating the subsidy of the CPR mainline," The Canadian Journal of Economics 24, 2 (1996), pg. 256.

10 Hugh G. J. Aitken, "Defensive Expansionism: The State and Economic Growth in Canada," in H. G. J. Aitken, ed, The State and Economic Growth (New York, Social Science Research Council, 1959). Pg. 80.

governments sought to thwart American commercial interests with a process that culminated with the creation of the CBC, the building of the CPR was a democratic imperative. British Columbia's entry into Confederation was contingent on the rail line being built. To have failed to deliver on this promise may have evinced a strong reaction from B.C. politicians, even leading to their withdrawal from Confederation. Nonetheless, a substantive, and therefore not to be discounted subtext, were the potential ambitions of American politicians, who harboured ideas of claiming portions of the Canadian West as their own.

Though the CPR was built during the 1881-1885 period, the crown corporation responsible for its oversight was not established until 1922. No fewer than 200 rail companies went insolvent, prompting the federal government to intervene in the national interest. Thus, the Canadian National Railway Company's (CNR) emergence came at a time when few thought there was any real and imminent territorial threat to Canada. It was borne by private enterprise's ineptitude and the need to maintain a railway for the national transportation of goods and persons. It became the first crown corporation in Canada.

The economic impetus for creating the CRN has not gone unchallenged. There have been assertions that this particular public enterprise initiative was an act of political sovereignty.[11] As seen from this light, nationalization of the railways was an act of predestination, and that private enterprise could have been part of the solution. The deeper one delves, the more apparent that there are unique and particular circumstances to the creation of crown corporations and also variable constants. The triggers for their creation via the federal order of government in Canada have been an apprehended threat to Canadian sovereignty (cultural, territorial, or economic), and a perception that private enterprise lacked the commitment and the capacity to supply what was needed.

---

11 Anthony Perl, "Public Enterprise as an Expression of Sovereignty: Reconsidering the Origin of Canadian National Railways," *Canadian Journal of Political Science* 27, 1 (1994), pgs. 25 & 26.

What the foregoing implies is the presence of an overall
public good that acts as a type of bedrock justification for the
existence of crown corporations. The public good in question
could be an essential service, such as a national railway line,
or a temporal device meant to meet an emergency, such as
crown corporations that have been created at times of war.
Concerning the latter, Polymer Corporation was enacted in 1942
to address the lack of supply of rubber, deemed essential for
the Canadian government's military efforts. In time, a private
company could have emerged to provide the materials but for
a nation in the throes of World War Two, urgency was of the
essence.[12] To be explicitly clear, the public good in question
with the above example was security, something that benefited
the broader public during the tensions of a world conflict.
The temporary nature of wartime crown corporations meant
that the lines between they and government departments
were blurred, even to the extent of some personnel holding
positions with both varieties of institutions simultaneously.[13]

Without devolving into an arcane discussion of public good
theory,[14] suffice is to say that proponents of crown corporations
believe that societal outcomes are enhanced with the existence
of these entities. Curiously, a public good such as the attainment
of knowledge may be wrapped up in what is tantamount to
a public-private partnership (at the post-secondary level),
but a related institution that carries out the disbursement of
scholarships (e.g. Millennium Scholarship Fund) falls under the
rubric of a crown corporation. In this case the public good is in
part facilitated, but not delivered, by corporations of the crown.

If one accepts the premise that government intervention exists
in practically every industry then it becomes a question of what

---

12 Matthew J. Bellamy, *Profiting the Crown: Canada's Polymer Corporations, 1942-1990*
    (Montreal, Quebec & Kingston, Ontario: McGill-Queen's University Press, 2005). Pg. xi.

13 Sandford F. Borins, "World War II Crown Corporations: Their Functions and Their Fate,"
    in J.R.S. Prichard, ed, *Crown Corporations in Canada: The Calculus of Instrumental
    Choice* (Toronto: Butterworths, 1983). Pg. 449.

14 J. Daniel Hammond, "Paul Samuelson on Public Goods: The Road to Nihilism,"
    History of Political Economy 47, 1 (2015), pgs. 149 & 150.

gradation of involvement is appropriate. The economic concept
of non-excludability is instructive. This term, when applied to
crown corporations, means that by providing a public good,
such entities do so because it is necessary to offer services that
the market can't logically justify. Utilities are one area where
it's necessary to have basic amenities available for citizens.
Water delivery regimes in Ontario and Michigan have had
disastrous consequences for public health namely because of
the lack of sufficient regulation and privatization. In addition
to the foregoing, such goods require a huge capital start-up
investment that private enterprise is unwilling to take on.[15]

In addition to striving for self-sufficiency, crown corporations also
operate on a parallel track because they are instruments of public
policy.[16] The duel imperative means there must be reporting
to legislative bodies who direct the latter, if not the former.
Beyond forensic accounting procedures that crown corporations
undergo, there must be a responsibility to both the legislative and
executive branches of government. Regardless of the order of
government, elected representatives must have the opportunity
to scrutinize the actions of these entities and to put questions to
the government as to their operation and appropriateness. Just
as importantly, cabinet ministers (and their deputies) must be
briefed regularly and be aware of changing circumstances that
crown corporations find themselves in.[17] Traditionally, cabinet
ministers are responsible for CC's inasmuch as their careers have
been on the line if troubles and or corruption entered public
consciousness. This produced an incentive in the system for active
oversight and accountability. Recent Canadian governments
have not closely adhered to the concept of ministerial
responsibility which may have future negative ramifications
for the reporting and operation of these organizations.

---

15 Edward M. Iacobucci and Michael J. Trebilcock, *The Role of Crown Corporations in the Canadian Economy* (Calgary, Alberta: School of Public Policy, University of Calgary, 2012). Pg. 2.

16 Tara Gray, *Crown Corporations and Governance and Accountability Framework: A Review of Recently Proposed Reforms* (Ottawa, Ontario: Library of Parliament, Parliamentary Research Service, 2006). Pgs. 1 & 2.

17 H.S. Gordon, "The Bank of Canada in a System of Responsible Government," *The Canadian Journal of Economics and Political Science* 27, 1 (1961), pg. 2.

A further upside to crown corporations is that they present the democratic process with institutional certainty,[18] meaning they help entrench the rules of the game. Between reporting to legislative and executive branches of government and conducting their affairs in (mostly) predictable ways, CC's contribute some measure of consistency to democracies. While institutional uncertainty is regarded as bad for democracy, uncertainty as to political outcomes is to be encouraged because it infuses the democratic system with alternate voices and public policy options.

The pathway from institutional design, to regular prescribed reportage, followed by democratic accountability looks impressive at first blush. After all, democratic accountability is a sacred cow in democratic societies and to obviate it to any prolonged and great extent is to invite eventual political mayhem. The term itself is defined as follows: "...is the accountability of decision-makers to the electoral forum: if voters are satisfied with governmental performance they will renew their mandate to the incumbents (positive consequence), and if not they will 'throw the rascals out (negative consequence)."[19] So, the implicit conceit in the term is that there is always a safety valve to ameliorate any operational shortcomings. Between the doctrine of ministerial responsibility and the ultimate hammer held by the voting populate, the contention is that crown corporations are systematically accountable with the implication that they are rigorous in the conduct of their affairs given the degree of scrutiny they undergo.

Another reason cited for the salience and importance of creating and maintaining crown corporations is their purported stabilizing effect from an economic standpoint. There are parts of Canada that have been underdeveloped and not enjoyed prosperity relative to the larger population centers. The attendant social

18 Adam Habib and Collette Schultz-Herzenberg, "Accountability and Democracy: Is the Ruling Elite Responsible to the Citzenry," in R. Calland and P. Graham, eds, *Democracy in the Time of Mbeki* (Cape Town, South Africa: Institute for Democracy in South Africa, 2005). Pgs. 167 & 168.

19 Yannis Papadopoulos, "Accountability and Multi-Level Governance: More Accountability, Less Democracy?" Revised version of a paper presented at the "Connex" workshop on Accountability, European University Institute, Florence, Italy, April 21, 2008. Pg. 3

and economic dislocation arising from this inequality has been deemed unacceptable and herein lie the importance of CC's as an instrument of public policy. At one stage in the country's economic evolution, they were also seen as a tool of modernization because they could serve the purpose of helping to address longstanding and deep-seated economic disparity. If, for instance, there was the prospect of an important plant closure in a one-industry town in a less than well off part of the country, a government could intervene by creating a crown corporation that would potentially stabilize the situation.[20] The neo-liberal epoch that we are experiencing acts as a type of break or discouragement to pursuing such action. Nevertheless, it is a tool that governments could enact if they so choose.

Further demonstration that crown corporations are a public policy device is evidenced by the claim that they provide stable employment during boom and bust economic cycles. Not only is re-numeration relatively stable, crown corporations have been singled out as a place where regulations that are meant to inject a modicum of employment equity exists, at least within federal CC's. *The Employment Equity Act of 1986* stipulated that women, Aboriginal peoples, persons with disabilities and visible minorities be given "a proportionate degree of representation in the workplace."[21] Therefore, advocates of crown corporations see them as important institutions that, in addition to performing the vital role that they've been assigned, also ensure built-in fairness by virtue of hiring practices that are given oversight by Parliament.

Between their aspirational roles at closing the regional disparity gap, their promotion of addressing longstanding employment inequity, and their modernization and stabilization during market-driven down cycles that can be periodically destructive, crown corporations are seen by their proponents to act as a calming economic influence.

---

20 M.J. Trebilcock and J.R.S. Prichard, *Crown Corporations: The Calculus of Instrument Choice* (Toronto: Butterworths, 1983). Pgs. 58 & 59.

21 Anonymous, "Employment Equity in the Federal Sector: A Progress Report," *The Worklife Report* 9, 3 (1994), pg. 1.

Process, Performance Considerations
and Potential for Abuse

The idea of what constitutes a crown corporation is further
defined in most circles as an entity that is "(1) at least 50%
owned by government; (2) incorporated under legislative or
company acts; (3) be normally separate from the government
as employers; (4) have boards of directors, some of which
(if not all of whose members are entitled to be appointed
by government; (5) emphasize the pursuit of profits as
part of their mandate; (6) compete with private-sector
companies in marketing their outputs."[22] From an institutional
design standpoint, these entities are fairly consistent.

The Canadian Constitution stakes out the operational spheres for
two orders of government, federal and provincial. The third order,
municipal, is disparaged frequently by being referred to as the
"creature" of provincial governments. Their lack of standing in the
ultimate law document is a source of ongoing consternation for
local government and urban planners alike. While the Constitution
stipulates specific areas of responsibility, there is also considerable
departmental overlap (e.g. health and fisheries) Additionally,
emergent fields of endeavour (e.g. technology and the environment)
raise their heads, calling for jurisdictional definition. Occasionally,
one of the orders of government will transfer oversight to another.
This was the case with gaming when the federal government
handed the regulatory regime to the provinces in 1985.[23]

There is a concomitant constitutional correlation to the
specific type of crown corporations that are created by
which order of government. For instance, the federal order
has jurisdiction over broadcasting. Therefore, it created
and oversees the CBC, even though the latter has an
arms length relationship with its Board of Directors.

---

22 Douglas F. Stevens, *Corporate Autonomy and Institutional Control: The Crown Corporation as a
    Problem in Organizational Design* (Montreal, Quebec and Kingston, Ontario: McGill-Queen's University
    Press, 1993). Pg. 51.

23 Garry J. Smith and Colin S. Campbell, "Tensions and Contentions: An Examination of Electronic Gaming
    Issues in Canada," *American Behavioral Scientist* 51, 1 (2007), pg. 88.

Provincial crown corporations in Canada are vast. It's been
estimated that over 200 exist but because the creation and
termination of these entities occurs on an ongoing basis,
delineating precisely how many exist at any given moment is
a challenge. Another problem lies in the notion that different
provinces have differing definitions of what constitutes a crown
corporation. This leads to a blurring between crown corporations
and governmental departments. The specified administration
of funds (e.g. – development corporations) could be included
among their number but in some jurisdictions entities such as
library boards fall under their ambit, thus the suggestion that they
are more of a government department has acquired saliency.[24]

As has been addressed earlier, the commercial performance
of crown corporations has traditionally taken a back seat to
the public policy aims and objectives of the governments that
own them. However, despite a recent spate of privatizations
of CC's, they still contribute 3.4% to the national GDP.[25] In the
event that crown corporations aren't commercial world-beaters,
politicians tend to emphasize the public good (e.g. job creation)
that arises from their existence, but the moment they begin to
turn a profit, elected officials tend to fall over themselves in a
bid to take credit for its success.[26] At the federal and provincial
level, the highest proliferation of CC's seemed to occur in the
1970s and 1980s while the municipal order's proclivity to create
crown corporations appears to be in a current upswing.

Corruption in crown corporations has been a longstanding
grievance. The wrong-doing inevitably stemmed from the
desire of politicians to influence or have a say in the day-to-day
operations of the organization in question. Observers say the

---

24 Aidan R. Vining and Robert Botterell, "An Overview of the Origins, Growth, Size and Functions of
     Provincial Crown Corporations," in J.R.S. Prichard, ed, *Crown Corporations in Canada: The Calculus of
     Instrument Choice* (Toronto: Butterworths, 1983). Pg. 305.

25 Daria Crisan and Kenneth J. McKenzie, "Government Owned Enterprises in Canada," *The School of
     Public Policy Research Papers* 6, 8 (2013), pg. 26.

26 Douglas F. Stevens, *Corporate Autonomy and Institutional Control: The Crown Corporation as a
     Problem in Organizational Design* (Montreal, Quebec and Kingston, Ontario: McGill-Queen's University
     Press, 1993). Pg. 109.

single biggest change with the governance of CC's is that governments have largely been practicing an arms length relationship with them in the modern epoch. For example, the Ontario Liqour Board was once rife with patronage appointments and ordering supplies was predicated on factors other than business rationale. Furthermore, mechanisms have been constructed to explicitly prevent the interference of politicians. For instance, the provincial government's shares in B.C. Ferries are held by a holding company. This measure is specifically aimed to prohibit interference in the daily operations of the public entity.[27]

Outright bribery has only become frowned upon in a serious way within the scope of the last 25 years. Canadian companies were permitted to engage in this practice as late as 1993. Crown corporations were able to justify bribery as part of their business plan in order to procure foreign contracts.[28] It is unclear whether the culture within federal crown corporations that enabled this practice had widespread acceptance for domestic purposes.

Beyond the foregoing, it would be unwise to omit the possibility that crown corporations are impacted by political transitions in the aftermath of general elections. Especially in cases where parties that have been absent from power for a considerable length of time, or just as pertinent, entering government for the first time, there is an understandable desire to put their stamp on governance. When world-view, perspective, and ideology are factored in, possibilities for alteration in the administration and orientation of crown corporations becomes heightened.

One especially compelling case study was Saskatchewan where in 1982 the incoming Devine Conservatives had an oft-pronounced disdain for the role of government and crown corporations, whereas their predecessors, the Blakeney New Democrats, envisioned an active and expansive role for these organizations.

---

27 Malcolm J. Bird, "The Embedded Crowns: The Evolution of Three Provincial State-Owned Enterprises," *Canadian Political Science Review* 9, 2 (2015), pg. 7.

28 A.W. Craig, "Business, Globalization, and the Logic and Ethics of Corruption," in J.D. Bishop, ed, *Ethics and Capitalism* (Toronto: University of Toronto Press, 2000). Pg. 126.

More explicitly, "to the NDP, the crown corporations represented a crucial component of a socialist strategy of development. To the Conservatives, crown corporations represented an overextended intrusion into the economy."[29] At first blush, the gulf between these two ideological positions seems insurmountable. However, what constitutes public rhetoric is often aimed at affecting an electoral result and does not reflect the ardent desire for structural or systematic change. Indeed, in the case of incoming governments, stability often depends on continuity in the make-up of the public service and crown corporations.

Again using the 1982 transition in Saskatchewan as an example, insinuations of patronage[30] were added to the dynamic with the end result being that the role of CC's were cast in disrepute by the Conservatives while in their previous incarnation as the Official Opposition. As is the case with all partisan political rhetoric there is a hue of truth to it. While CC's may not have become universal "resting homes"[31] for political allies that fell into disfavour by the electorate, patronage appointments were normalized. In the current epoch, obvious patronage appointments face severe blowback from a public impatient with outright malfeasance.

At odds with notions of meritocracy that had enveloped mid to late 20th century political culture in Canada, political patronage nonetheless enjoyed a central role within the political system. While the tolerance for overt incidences of patronage has largely dissipated, to believe that CC's do not practice patronage themselves or are instruments of patronage by partisan political actors would be naïve in the extreme. Appointments to the boards of crown corporations are invariably made by political actors[32] and as such, patronage

---

29 Hans J. Michelman and Jeffrey S. Steeves, "The 1982 transition to Power in Saskatchewan: The Progressive Conservatives and the Public Service," *Canadian Public Administration* 28, 1 (1985), pg. 12.

30 Saskatchewan, *Debates and Proceedings*, Fourth Session, Nineteenth Legislature, December 1st, 1981, pg. 9.

31 Hans J. Michelman and Jeffrey S. Steeves, "The 1982 transition to Power in Saskatchewan: The Progressive Conservatives and the Public Service," *Canadian Public Administration* 28, 1 (1985), pg. 5.

32 Reg Whitaker, "Between Patronage and Bureaucracy: Democratic Politics in Transition," *Journal of Canadian Studies* 22, 2 (1987), pg. 66.

avenues are opened up, although these organizations of recent vintage have "professionalized" the appointment process.

The history of democratic reform in Canada is laced with instances of critics lambasting governments for their unethical use of patronage. On democratic reformer Pierre Fliott Trudeau, repeatedly castigated the Duplessis government for its abuses of power. Tellingly, Trudeau and other democratic reformers refrained from directing his ire at crown corporations. On the one hand, his blindness to the subject predates the full-scale proliferation of CC's in the two decades after his ascension to the prime minister-ship. It may also reveal a desire on the part of Trudeau to go easy on crown corporations so that he himself could utilize them as instruments of patronage. Indeed, under his watch, they became "the nesting place for clearly partisan appointees."[33]

Despite previous claims to more enlightened approaches, the headlines of current affairs news coverage are rife with allegations of patronage appointments to boards of federal crown corporations. Directors, CEOs and Chairs of CC's, because of their high profile nature and because they are appointed by elected officials, are susceptible to claims of patronage. Of particular concern were the actions of the recently defeated Conservative government that chose to reappoint its favorites for terms that extended for years into the current government's mandate,[34] preventing the overriding claim of democratic accountability from manifesting itself. For if it is claimed that one aspect of accountability in the system is that governments must answer for their appointments to crown corporations, and if those appointments were made by the previous regime, such accountability is severely obviated. One member of a provincial legislature opined that appointments to crown corporations should require a two-thirds affirmative vote for them to take affect.[35]

---

33 Jeffrey Simpson, "The Two Trudeaus: Federal Patronage in Quebec, 1968-84," *Journal of Canadian Studies* 22, 2 (1987), pg. 98.

34 Elizabeth Thompson, "Doomed Harper Government Made 49 'Future' Patronage Appointments," *iPolitics*, November 23, 2015, viewed at: http://ipolitics.ca/2015/11/23/doomed-harper-government-made-49-future-patronage-appointments/

35 Denis Perron, "Roundtable: Patronage and the Scrutiny of Appointments," *Canadian Parliamentary Review* 1986. Viewed at: http://www.revparl.ca/english/issue.asp?art=711¶m=120

Some have imagined that crown corporations could combine the best of both private innovation and public accountability:

If we establish the public corporation, it must be for certain reasons. What are they? They are that we seek to combine the principles of public accountability…with the liveliness, initiative, and a considerable degree of the freedom that is quick-moving and progressive business enterprise. Either that is the case for a public corporation or there is no case at all.[36]

As the foregoing hints at, therein lies the rub: the balancing act between autonomy and accountability may preclude either aspect of crown corporations from being fully-realized. It may well be that innovations such as delegative democracy might expedite accountability or transfer it to a more nimble and easy-attained model. Traditionally, the autonomy/accountability continuum has been an attempt at achieving a balancing act, although its achievement has been at times dubious. A 1974 examination of crown corporations in Ontario revealed they enjoyed "a great deal of autonomy, were created in an unsystematic and *ad hoc* fashion with a low level of interaction with other government activities, and were often funded without detailed scrutiny."[37] Subsequent reforms in that province have brought things back into a state of relative equilibrium.

More recently, clearer attempts have been made by governmental stakeholders to at least give the impression that accountability takes precedence in the formation of, and reportage by, crown corporations. Some provinces, British Columbia to name but one, have tried to establish conflict-of-interest guidelines for board members. These guidelines can be ignored, altered, or flaunted by succeeding governments and in an age when media scrutiny is

36 Charles Allan Ashley and Reginald George Hampden Smails, *Canadian Crown Corporations: Some Aspects of Their Administration and Control* (Toronto: Macmillan Co. of Canada Limited, 1965). Pg. 3.

37 Joanne Pawluk, *An Introduction to Alberta's Crown Corporations*, Legislative Internship Paper, June 1984. Pg. 14.

diminishing, the public may often not be alert to such crucial shortcomings. Also, there are scenarios by which board appointments may be made with merit and skills criteria simply overridden in the interests of political patronage.

If boards are to provide adequate oversight into the overall direction of crown corporations, getting clear signals from the governments they report to is essential. Mandate letters, Shareholders Letters of Expectations, and Memoranda of Understanding[38] designed to spell out the aims and objectives of CC's are devices that modern governments now utilize. These documents are essential because they describe important public policy objectives, responsibilities, and identify the powers of its board. Moreover, these slight innovations should militate against, but not eliminate, the possibility of overarching misunderstanding that previously was a mainstay in the relationship between the crown and its public corporations. Their existence may also make it more likely that governments can detect "end arounds" or instances where crown corporations are running amuck or in defiance of the expectations of democratically-elected legislatures and Ministers.

Concomitantly, it is increasingly demanded that senior officers within crown corporations certify[39] to the carrying out of their specified responsibilities. This measure is intended to further entrench accountability into the governance culture of crown corporations. If abject falsehoods arise from such certifications, the organization's officers are much more likely to be found out. While such a safeguard does not transfer responsibility from politically-appointed actors, it does ensure a paper trail through which subsequent investigation can either confirm or not confirm the accuracy of the declarations.

---

38 Allison Dempsey and Jacques Levesque, "Governance of Crown Agencies," *Proceedings of the March 2005 Conference, March 10-11, 2005, Vancouver, B.C.* (Toronto: Conference Board of Canada, 2005), pg. 4.

39 Treasury Board of Canada Secretariat, *Meeting the Expectations of Canadians: Review of the Governance Framework*, Report to Parliament (Ottawa, Ontario: Treasury Board of Canada, 2005), pg. 35.

When, on November 11, 1947, Winston Churchill said "…it has been said that democracy is the worst form of government except for all those other forms that have been tried from time to time…"[40] he wasn't conferring finality on the democratic project that has consumed great and lesser minds since ancient Greece. Inherent in this oft-quoted remark is belief that there is much room for improvement and that despite immense despair and frustrations that democracy produces, its transitory template is still worthy of our attention.

In the context of crown corporations, the question might be - how can we better their governance and expand democratic control? It should be said up front that in posing such a question, there is no expectation of coming up with a *de facto* replacement for representative democracy. While it is true that, on one level, elected representatives could be considered proxies, their responsibilities extend well beyond that of showing up and casting ballots in legislative forums. They also act as advocates on behalf of groups and individuals, and their offices are frequently engaged in answering a bevy of requests by constituents who seek simple information or look for guidance on how to navigate the political system. In short, it would be a serious error to equate representative democracy with delegative democracy because each has dimensions that may not be apparent at first look.

One also occasionally sees proxy voting connected to direct democracy. The three aspects that comprise direct democracy are referenda, the ballot initiative, and recall. So, in this context, applying proxy voting to the conduct of crown corporations seems non-applicable. Just to be clear, there is no one version of democracy that encompasses all of human needs and wants.

---

40 Winston Churchill, U.K. House of Commons, November 11, 1947.

If one views democracy exclusively as a decision-making device, it can obviously be made better. Representative democracy has been examined and found wanting by political scientists.[41] Whether it be the sage scions of Greece meeting in The Forum, New Englanders casting votes in town meetings, or the Westminster parliamentary model employed by Canada and other countries, the transconfiguration of democracy is ongoing. Rather than treating representative democracy as an immovable object, it would be wise to see it as a potentially complimentary component to proxy voting or delegative democracy.

A potential drawback of proxy voting is the notion that because it values the participation of those who enjoy cognition and awareness of issues and political processes, it could be viewed as a brake on civic literacy[42] by incidentally encouraging those who are not familiar with issues to remain unawares. Proxy voting is not necessarily a device that lifts up the entire population's civic capacity. Instead, it recognizes that in an imperfect world, it is desirable and necessary to have those who are informed be at the fore of democratic decision making.

Canadian political parties have practiced a form of delegative democracy when it came to the selection of party leaders who were chosen by delegates selected by party members in constituency or riding associations. In effect, party members trusted one another to follow through on their stated intentions as enunciated at local meetings. The delegates acted on behalf of those who could not be physically present at the time and place of the actual leadership convention. Recently, this practice has dissipated or given way to a one-vote/one member formula. So, if anything, formal institutional politics in Canada has witnessed a decline in delegative democracy.

---

41 Paul Hirst, Representative Democracy and Its Limits, *The Political Quarterly* 59, 2 (1988), pgs. 1 & 2. See also, Alan Rosenthal, *The Decline of Representative Democracy: Process, Participation, and Power in State Legislatures* (Washington, D.C.: CQ Press, 1998).

42 Defined as "The knowledge and ability capacity of citizens to make sense of their political world" in Henry Milner, *Civic Literacy: How Informed Citizens Make Democracy Work* (Hanover, Massachusetts: University Press of New England, 2002). Pg. 1.

The present absence of proxy voting in Canada's democratic institutions does not mean it will remain that way into perpetuity. The Swiss have been innovators in the area of direct democracy, to the point where elected representatives are more likely to take their cue from a populace that is mobilized regularly in an institutional regime that features national referenda. It may well be that proxy voting, whose chief feature is that it expands those charged with making public policy decisions, can arrive at a similar relationship with representative forms of democracy. In fact, the mandate of representatives could be theoretically strengthened if their actions are informed by decisions made by large numbers of proxy voters. What it would take on the part of elected representatives, is a willingness to share power with an increasing amount of their fellow citizens. In practical terms, such an eventuality would mean that these elected officials would have to adopt proposals for proxy-voting, or face defeat at the ballot box. Since politicians are especially fastidious in their propensity to share power,[43] there needs to be recognition on their part that democracy can be bettered and their own role legitimated, from a schema that involves proxy voting.

Proxy voting, because of its operational emphasis on quality and informed citizenry, may seem to potentially limit public participation (when compared to direct democracy). However, in actuality it would entail many more people making decisions. The key to its potential is to discover how elected representatives, legislatures, the executive branch and governmental organizations, including crown corporations can not just co-exist and augment one another, but strengthen democratic practice.

In the case of crown corporations how would the prospect of thousands of proxy voters alter its reality? In order for any theoretical concept to become operational, a model needs to be suggested and tried. For the purposes of this paper, I am proposing that Canada adopt a system of proxy voting or

---

43 James Mahoney and Kathleen Thelen, *Explaining Institutional Change: Ambiguity, Agency, and Power* (Cambridge, England: Cambridge University Press, 2009). Pg. xi.

delegative democracy[44] that provides additional oversight and helps to inform current political actors. The Canadian Assembly would consist of citizens that meet criteria that permit them to have authority to cast votes on matters of public policy and help to determine the scope of institutions such as crown corporations.

The Canadian Assembly, proxy voters all, would make decisions on issues. It may be that this Assembly has certain areas of endeavour that are manifestly off limits (judicial rulings, human rights, constitutional amendments, *etc.*). Bills in federal and provincial legislatures typically have three readings before they are given royal assent. After first reading, the proposed Bill is usually susceptible to alteration or amendment, being deferred to a parliamentary committee. What if elected representatives on these committees routinely submitted the Bills to the Canadian Assembly for input? The Committee could take its cue from a wide swath of the Canadian populace under the aegis of proxy voters. In this way, the decisions of Committee members could be strengthened by the votes taken by Canadian Assembly members. There would also be considerable pressure for the parliamentarians to adhere to the decisions made by their newfound democratic partners.

If enacted, the foregoing reform to the parliamentary system could potentially expand democratic decision making. Based on how well trial experiments unfold, further expansion of delegative democracy could be pursued. Potentially every Bill that comes before the House of Commons could be subject to a vote from the proxy-driven Canadian Assembly. If the latter body reaches a certain percentage voting threshold, the Bill is enacted, whereas if it falls below the stipulated threshold, the parliamentarians hold sway and the fate of the Bill resides in their collective hands. Such a formula would ensure an ongoing place for representative democracy while simultaneously expanding the powers of the people within the broader democratic society.

---

44 Bryan Ford, *Delegative Democracy* 2002, viewed at: http://www.brynosaurus.com/log/2002/0515-DelegativeDemocracy.pdf

Returning to the question of crown corporations, how should proxy-voting or delegative democracy interact with such entities? The answer to that question may lie be found by returning to the primary purposes of the crown corporations to begin with: (1) to fulfill a role in the implementation of public policy; (2) to carry out the business mandate of corporations by providing goods or services that are efficiently delivered. Under the proposal articulated above, there could be a role for the Canadian Assembly to be played in providing another layer of oversight. For instance, annual reports go before the Assembly for scrutiny. Also, in the event that Parliament happens to be between sittings and the crown corporation in question requires democratic input because they propose to do something outside of the scope of their business plan, the Assembly could serve the role of a sounding board.

Annual reports are one of the ways crown corporations purport to be made accountable to legislators, regardless of the order of government. This provision, at least federally, can be attributed to the recommendations of the Lambert Commission.[45] It also called on the Minister to conduct a re-evaluation of specific crown corporations once every ten years to determine their present and future prospects. It is possible that proxy-voters could play a role in triggering a review at intervals lesser than the mandated ten years, especially if the crown corporation are in trouble or straying from ethical practices. In other words, there should be a mechanism in place that enables the Canadian Assembly to inveigh on the conduct or direction of crown corporations. This would not necessarily impinge on the ability of the crown corporation

---

45 M.J. Trebilcock and J.R.S. Prichard, *Crown Corporations: The Calculus of Instrument Choice* (Toronto: Butterworths, 1983). Pg. 79.

boards of directors to act within their prescribed instructions from government and to carry out their responsibilities. Proxy-voters would have to meet carefully laid-out criteria that still allows for the CC in question to have relative autonomy.

The foregoing implies that present actors within crown corporations would have to be cognizant of the advantages and disadvantages of either initiating a submission to proxy voters or conversely, under some circumstances, having to grapple with an oversight process initiated by proxy voters. What at first blush could be regarded as a nuisance or inconvenience could be highly beneficial to crown corporations because they would still have the imperative of steering the proverbial ship, ensuring that the CC meets statutory and legislative requirements, and providing oversight for its day-to day operations. All this would not be altered. Changed would be the addition of another, broader body of people that could give its assent to the overall mission of the CC in question and provide informed feedback at the first sign of trouble. This would serve to strengthen their overall mandate and at the same time place a safety value in the system that does not exist presently.

It is important to point out that the Canadian Assembly or comparable provincial or municipal entities would not cancel out the need for other institutional checks on crown corporations. Entities such as Attorney-Generals or Solicitor-Generals would continue to exercise their required statutory and legislative responsibilities. Proxy voters would augment other systematic actors and add to the scrutiny and deliberative nature of the democratic process.

Conclusion

Despite low voter turnouts in recent decades, Canadians remain passionate about many aspects of politics. Crown corporations illicit particularly exercised debate because of their significant role as public policy and economic instruments. This paper has asserted that delegative democracy would be a means to improving the relationship of crown corporations to the citizenry and that the creation of a proxy-voting entity, the Canadian Assembly, would benefit democratic institutions that provide ongoing oversight to CC's.

The initial portion of the paper sought to articulate a casual pattern for their establishment in the Canadian context. The middle section was concerned with enunciating traits of their existence in a federated state and delving into the political corruption that has characterized part of their place in the body politic. The last section was more normative in nature, calling for the establishment of a delegative democracy model that seeks to augment representative democracy and, more specifically, crown corporations.

Bibliography

Aitken, Hugh G. J. "Defensive Expansionism: The State and Economic Growth in Canada." *The State and Economic Growth.* Ed. H. G. J. Aitken. New York: Social Science Research Council, 1959.

Anonymous. "Employment Equity in the Federal Sector: A Progress Report." *The Worklife Report.* 9, 3 (1994): 1-3.

Asheley, C.A., and Snails, Reginald George Hampden. *Canadian Crown Corporations: Some Aspects of Their Administration and Control.* Toronto: Macmillan and Company, 1965.

Bellamy, Matthew J. *Profiting the Crown: Canada's Polymer Corporations, 1942-1990.* Montreal, Quebec & Kingston, Ontario: McGill-Queen's University Press, 2005.

Bird, Malcolm J. "The Embedded Crowns: The Evolution of Three Provincial State-Owned Enterprises." *Canadian Political Science Review.* 9, 2 (2015): 1-20.

Boardman, Anthony E., and Vining, Aidan R. "Public Service Broadcasting in Canada." *The Journal of Media Economics* 9, 1 (1996): 47-61.

Borins, Sandford F. "World War II Crown Corporations: Their Functions and Their Fate." *Crown Corporations in Canada: The Calculus of Instrumental Choice.* Ed. J.R.S. Prichard Toronto: Butterworths, 1983. 447-475.

Canada, House of Commons. *Debates.* May 31, 1928.

Churchill, Winston. *U.K. House of Commons.* November 11, 1947.

Craig, A.W. "Business, Globalization, and the Logic and Ethics of Corruption." *Ethics and Capitalism.* Ed. J.D. Bishop. Toronto: University of Toronto Press, 2000.

Crisan, Daria, and McKenzie, Kenneth J. "Government Owned Enterprises in Canada." *The School of Public Policy Research Papers.* 6, 8 (2013): 1-30.

Dempsey, Allison, and Levesque, Jacques. "Governance of Crown Agencies." *Proceedings of the March 2005 Conference, March 10-11, 2005, Vancouver, B.C.*

Emery, J.C. Herbert, and McKenzie, Kenneth J. "Damned if you do, Damned if you don't: an Option Value Approach to Evaluating the Subsidy of the CPR Mainline." *The Canadian Journal of Economics* 24, 2 (1996): 255-270.

Ford, Bryan. *Delegative Democracy.* 2002. Viewed at: http://www.brynosaurus.com/log/2002/0515-DelegativeDemocracy.pdf

Gray, Tara. *Crown Corporations and Governance and Accountability Framework: A Review of Recently Proposed Reforms.* Ottawa, Ontario: Library of Parliament, Parliamentary Research Service, 2006.

Gordon, H.S. "The Bank of Canada in a System of Responsible Government." *The Canadian Journal of Economics and Political Science.* 27, 1 (1961): 1-22.

Habib, Adam, and Schultz-Herzenberg, Collette. "Accountability and Democracy: Is the Ruling Elite Responsible to the Citizenry." *Democracy in the Time of Mbeki.* Eds. R. Calland and P. Graham. Cape Town, South Africa: Institute for Democracy in South Africa, 2005.

Hammond, J. Daniel. "Paul Samuelson on Public Goods: The Road to Nihilism." *History of Political Economy* 47, 1 (2015): 174-198.

Hirst, Paul. "Representative Democracy and Its Limits." *The Political Quarterly.* 59, 2 (1988): 190-205.

Hood, Christopher. "The 'New Public Management' in the 1980s: Variations on a Theme." *Accounting, Organization and Society* 20, 2/3 (1995): 93-109.

Iacobucci, Edward M., and Trebilcock, Michael J. *The Role of Crown Corporations in the Canadian Economy.* Calgary, Alberta: School of Public Policy, University of Calgary, 2012.

Mahoney, James, and Thelen, Kathleen. *Explaining Institutional Change: Ambiguity, Agency, and Power.* Cambridge, England: Cambridge University Press, 2009.

Michelman, Hans J., and Steeves, Jeffrey S. "The 1982 transition to Power in Saskatchewan: The Progressive Conservatives and the Public Service." *Canadian Public Administration.* 28, 1 (1985): 3-28.

Milner, Henry. *Civic Literacy: How Informed Citizens Make Democracy Work.* Hanover, Massachusetts: University Press of New England, 2002.

Papadopoulos, Yannis. "Accountability and Multi-Level Governance: More Accountability, Less Democracy?" Paper presented at the "Connex" workshop on Accountability, European University Institute, Florence, Italy, April 21, 2008.

Pawluk, Joanne. *An Introduction to Alberta's Crown Corporations.* Legislative Internship Paper, June 1984.

Perl, Anthony. "Public Enterprise as an Expression of Sovereignty: Reconsidering the Origin of Canadian National Railways." *Canadian Journal of Political Science* 27, 1 (1994): 23-52.

Perron, Denis. "Roundtable: Patronage and the Scrutiny of Appointments." *Canadian Parliamentary Review.* 1986. Viewed at: http://www.revparl.ca/english/issue.asp?art=711¶m=120

Plaunt Papers, E.H. Blake to Spry, March 13, 1931.

Prang, Margaret. "The Origins of Public Broadcasting in Canada." *Canadian Historical Review* 46, 1 (1965): 1-31.

Prichard, J. Robert S. *Crown Corporations in Canada: The Calculus of Instrument Choice.* Toronto: Butterworths, 1983.

Raboy, Marc. "The Role of Public Consultation in Shaping the

Canadian Broadcasting System." *Canadian Journal of Political Science* 28, 3 (1995): 455-477.

Rosenthal, Alan. *The Decline of Representative Democracy: Process, Participation, and Power in State Legislatures.* Washington, D.C.: CQ Press, 1998.

Saskatchewan. *Debates and Proceedings.* Fourth Session, Nineteenth Legislature, December 1st, 1981.

Simpson, Jeffrey. "The Two Trudeaus: Federal Patronage in Quebec, 1968-84." *Journal of Canadian Studies.* 22, 2 (1987): 96-110.

Smith, Garry J., and Campbell, Colin S. "Tensions and Contentions: An Examination of Electronic Gaming Issues in Canada." *American Behavioral Scientist.* 51, 1 (2007): 86-101.

Stevens, Douglas F. *Corporate Autonomy and Institutional Control: The Crown Corporation as a Problem in Organizational Design.* Montreal, Quebec and Kingston, Ontario: McGill-Queen's University Press, 1993.

Thompson, Elizabeth. "Doomed Harper Government Made 49 'Future' Patronage Appointments." *iPolitics* November 23, 2015. Viewed at: http://ipolitics.ca/2015/11/23/doomed-harper-government-made-49-future-patronage-appointments/

Treasury Board of Canada Secretariat. *Meeting the Expectations of Canadians: Review of the Governance Framework.* Report to Parliament. Ottawa, Ontario: Treasury Board of Canada, 2005.

Vining, Aidan R., and Botterell, Robert. "An Overview of the Origins, Growth, Size and Functions of Provincial Crown Corporations." *Crown Corporations in Canada: The Calculus of Instrument Choice.* Ed. J.R.S. Prichard. Toronto: Butterworths, 1983. 303-368.

Whitaker, Reg. "Between Patronage and Bureaucracy: Democratic Politics in Transition." *Journal of Canadian Studies.* 22, 2 (1987): 57-61.

Deep Democracy – Short Article

We in the West live in the democratic age—who could deny it? Our lives are governed by democratic governments, by democratic laws, and by democratic mores and manners. The democratic standard of equality is the ruling criterion of the day. Most criticism of democracy is that certain parts of society are not democratic enough. Consider only the recent debate in Canada surrounding reforming the electoral system, where the underlying question is, "Which system is *more* democratic?" The charges against the status quo are directed at further improving democracy by ever increasing the degree of equality: the democratization of democracy necessitates the universalization of equality. Could it be the case, however, that too much equality is bad for democracy?

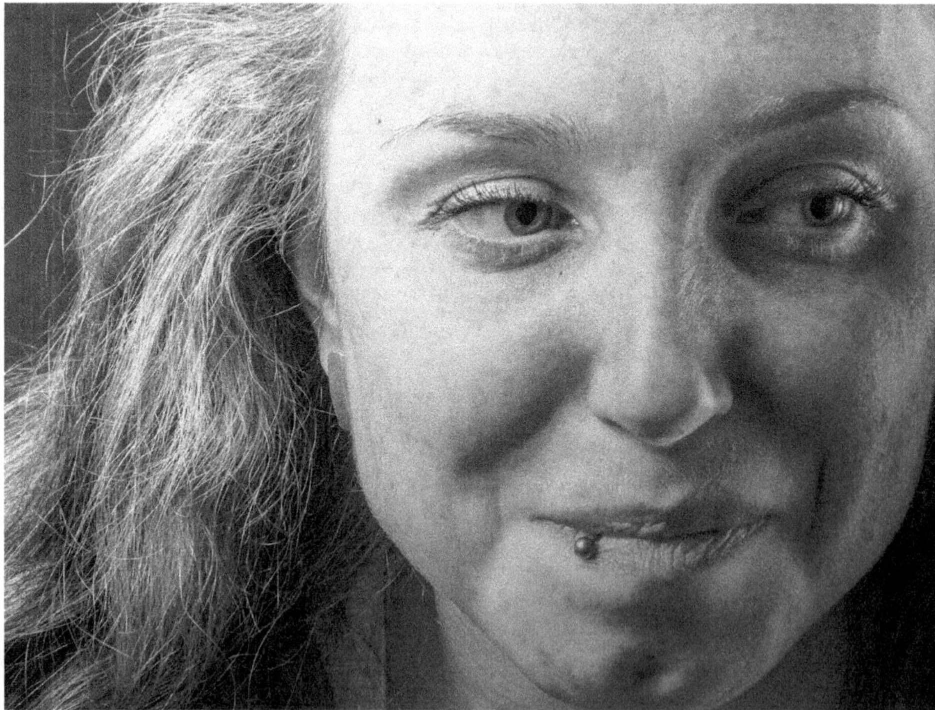

There is reason to believe that democracy is enhanced by certain non-democratic elements. Democracy is best served when natural inequalities—of knowledge, ability, resources, etc.—are left to flourish, at least to some degree. That is to say, the democratic ideal is better met when ineluctable inequalities aim to serve democracy itself. Certain technologies may help in this regard. Technology can direct discrepancies of various kinds towards the improvement of democracy, as well as mitigate inequalities so they remain within legitimate democratic parameters.

The aforementioned argument applies both to the broader societal level as well as to what can be considered a microcosm of democratic society, namely, the workplace. Workplaces today are prone to the same democratic tendencies as the rest of society; however, unlike the democratic regime at large, most workplaces retain an element of meritocracy. In other words, the workplace is imbued with a remnant of hierarchy somewhat inconsistent with the broader logic of pure equality. The workplace should retain—even embrace—this fact, and society at large can benefit from changes in workplace composition and practice. In fact, the workplace may serve as a locale for democratic experimentation.

The experiment proposed herein is the following: that voters ought to not only cast a vote in electing a representative, but that they should be able to delegate their vote to another. Insofar as voters already translate, or transfer, their will to a representative, a further mechanism allowing them to transfer their vote—or, inserting a "proxy" into the democratic arrangement—may have certain benefits. These include, the greater dissemination, collection, and application of information and knowledge; re-aligning democracy with the digital and information age; harvesting greater value, defined as human capital; rebuilding trust in institutions and officials; limiting possibilities for corruption; and so on.

One of the great difficulties—and critiques—of modern democracy is that there is an imbalance of knowledge or understanding, and that the electorate is either apathetic or uninterested in many political issues. Despite the great benefit of living in a society that has fought for freedoms, such as that of casting one's ballot, democratic societies have a tendency to drift—that is, to become prone to disengagement, or what is sometimes called "individualism," insofar as individuals turn inward and away from the broader society. There are many reasons for this, and certain broadly philosophic correctives proposed include enhancing civic education, strengthening liberal education and understanding, and the like, while certain policy-oriented corrective include making voting mandatory. However, it may be the case that modern democratic societies follow an *inevitable logic*, at least to some degree: that the democratization of democracy leads to de-politicization among the electorate.

Insofar as modern democracies impose no great responsibilities upon the citizenry, the citizenry is left to pursue its private endeavors. The liberation of the private realm from public impositions enlarges the private sphere—the expansion of the latter occurs to the detriment of the latter. While some of the correctives have validity, and ought to be encouraged, the best approaches may be those that accept some of the inevitability of democratic drift. This is not to say that democrats ought to give up on their fellow citizens, but that citizenship should be redefined, and that democratic practices need to be reconsidered.

Certain forms of delegative democracy offer practices worthy of such consideration. Properly understood, delegative democracy works *within* the democratic logic while working *against* its negative tendencies. Rather than standing athwart to historical trends, delegative democracy can realistically guide the best of democracy without falling prey to high-minded ideals of democracy otherwise out of reach—the pure schemes dreamt up by democratic theorists. In order to engage in the practice of delegative democracy, certain technologies are necessary, some of which are beginning to be available today.

Delegative democracy re-envisions the relationship between the citizenry and its leadership as a dialogic relationship, one defined by authentic dialogue between the two parties, or between the various elements of governance. A voter's delegate in such a system may not be a stranger but instead one's friend, colleague of family member, or otherwise someone one deems to be more experienced or better acquainted with and informed on an issue. The individual acquiring the vote of their fellow becomes their delegate—a representative through the power of their vote. Citizens can communicate with their delegates at a level of directness, and at any point if the delegate fails to adequately or ethically represent, the position of delegate can be revoked with little effort. Thus, this relationship plays to the natural strengths and resources of individuals—certain inherent inequalities—without letting these things run amok—without inequalities becoming anti-democratic.

The key element in this relationship is trust, as trust must be developed by delegates in order to represent individuals in their vote. The arrangement therefore improves faith in governance by developing and leveraging quality relationships (potential and extant) between voters and delegates. And on a larger societal level, rather than having a limited ballot of officially sanctioned candidates to choose from, voter confidence would improve with citizens selecting the best individual to represent them from their communities. Imagine a technology that could not only help facilitate and build trust, but could likewise measure and value it; a technology that would allow for the improved allocation and dissemination of information for improved performance and outcome on decision making; a technology that would improve democratic practices by enacting the principles of delegative democracy. This is just the technology outlined below, and that is presently being developed.

Technologies first emerge on a small scale, and in the incipient stages they are often applied experimentally in controlled settings. To reiterate what was said above, the workplace offers a beneficial and readily available space for experimentation. The technology in mind…

"Children possess knowledge and opinions about their lives and experiences that may differ from those ascribed to them by adults. However, on too many occasions they are not consulted. Adults often assume that they know what children are thinking and feeling and so do not ask for their input when making decisions about matters that concern them. Adults need to listen to children in order to claim to speak on their behalf. If not, the decisions they make for children may have negative rather than positive consequences." PAUL STEPHENSON

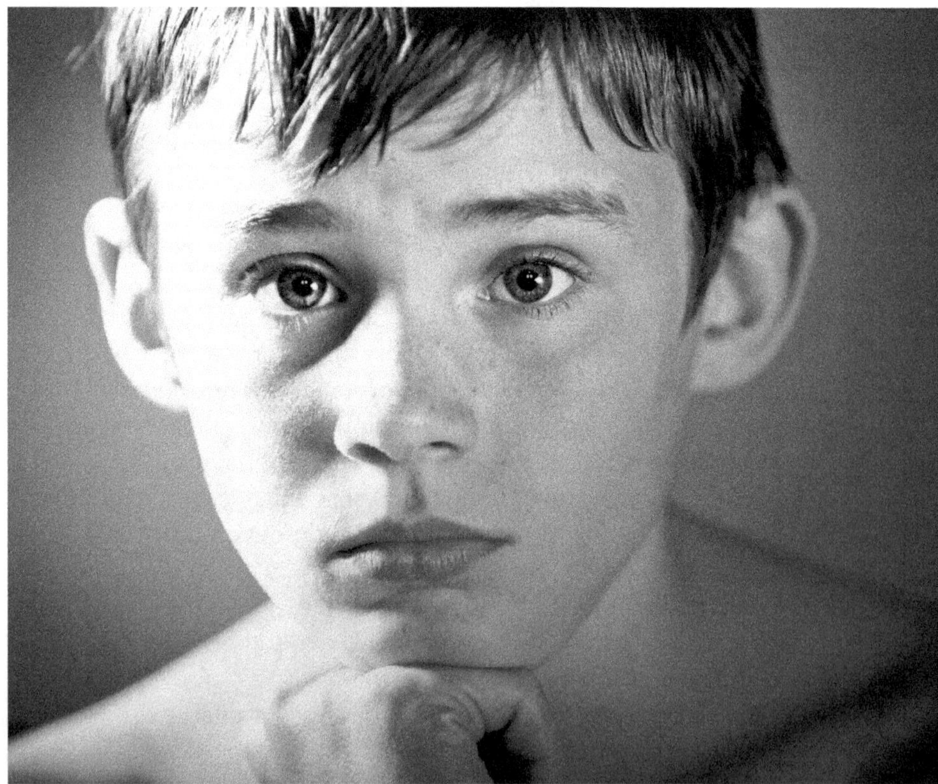

Children's Suffrage and
the Proxy Voting Solution

Suffrage is political franchise, the right to vote in a public election. When modern democracy began approximately two centuries ago, only rich landowning white men held this privilege to vote. Gradually, this right has been extended to minorities such as other races, women and the poor. There is still one group, however, that is notably missing…children[1]. Many view the lack of political voice for children as a modern day injustice in the same way it was for minorities and women. And just as these historical minorities fought and eventually won their right to vote, advocates have been calling for voting reform for children.

At first glance, our children's lack of participation in democracy may seem acceptable simply because it has been the normalized experience of most voters. However, once we take a close look at the impact this has on children if we view them as human beings with their own set of rights, we may begin to glimpse it as one of the blind injustices of our generation. The majority of public decisions affecting children, both in government and civil society are made without their active participation. This means that neither their views nor their inputs are heard.

Children are the forgotten constituency of the modern era. In many developed countries around the world, a higher standard of living, modern health care and improved diets have resulted in extending the average human lifespan. This has resulted in a significant growth in the elderly population. Meanwhile, fertility rates in these same countries have plummeted. There is a close relationship between these major demographic trends and the rights of children.

---

1   In this book, we adopt the terminology used in the 1989 *Convention on the Rights of the Child*, which defines the Child as *every human being below the age of eighteen*. We use children and child interchangeably.

Total Fertility and proportion of global
population 1970-1975 to 2035-2030

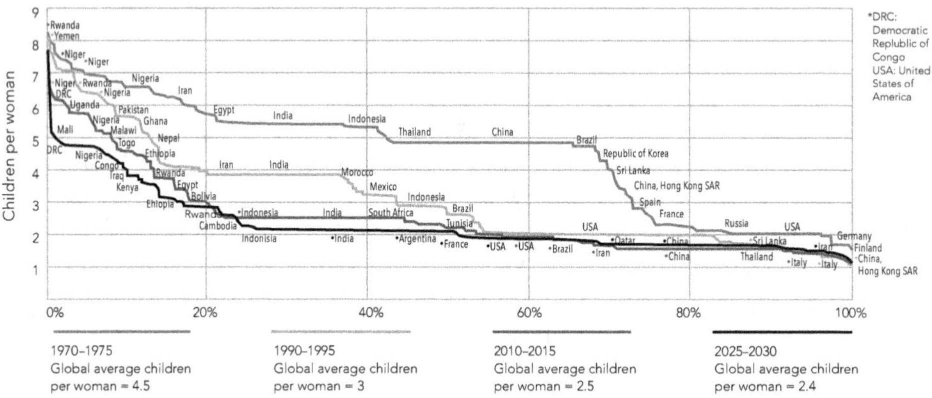

1970–1975	1990–1995	2010–2015	2025–2030
Global average children per woman = 4.5	Global average children per woman = 3	Global average children per woman = 2.5	Global average children per woman = 2.4

(UN, World Fertility Patterns 2015, 2015)

Since children are disenfranchised to the degree that they have no right to vote, whilst the elderly capture an increasing share of the adult votes, policy and the resultant resource allocations thereof is skewed in favor of the needs of the elderly. In 1992, using United States data from 1959 to 1990, political scientist Paul Peterson demonstrated this connection between policy and impacts on children and the elderly. His research clearly showed how the greater share of the elderly vote resulted in policies that favored the elderly, taking a bigger piece of the social welfare pie for their use, at the same time decreasing the share for children.

Poverty rates and funding for elderly and children,
United States 1950 to 1990.

	Children	Elderly
Poverty rate: 1959	14 %	35 %
Poverty rate: 1990	21 %	11 %
Health Funding: 2010	$10 billion	$435 billion

(Peterson, 1992)

In a 2004 paper, Newacheck and Benjamin summarized their research between the elderly and children population in the US, noting a significant divergence in social spending between 1965 and 2000. This data correlates with Peterson's research showing the proportional shifts in poverty rates between these two demographics. Newacheck and Benjamin argue that social welfare spending for children and elders is driven more by political reasons and macroeconomic trends than the real needs of the two populations and call for a new doctrine of fairness to ensure that vulnerable populations are not force to compete for resources (Newacheck & Benjamin, 2004).

TABLE 2

Poverty rates and funding for elderly and children, United States 1950 to 1990

Social Spending	Children	Elderly
1965	37 %	21 %
1986	25 %	33 %

(Newacheck & Benjamin, 2004)

The net result of current demographic trends is to further erode the already tenuous rights of children. The political system needs to change to reflect the real needs of the changing demographics. In spite of the noble voices of the elderly who proclaim concern for the younger generation, research shows that the opposite is in fact the case. The reality today is that children suffer immensely for lack of representation. For a country such as the United States that built its constitution on taxation with representation, it speaks volumes that 75 million citizens or 25% of the population is taxed without representation. Globally, the figure is even worse; children comprise a third of the world's population (UN, 2015).

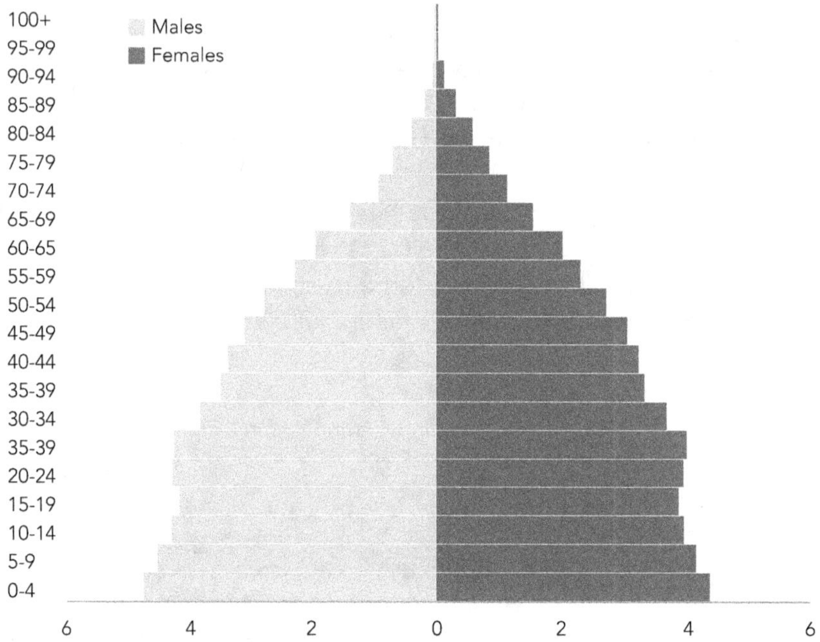

(Source: UN Dept of Economic and Social Affairs, Population Division 2015. World Population Prospects: The 2015 Revision)

If children were allowed to vote, could their representation correct the current political imbalances that emerge from imbalanced representation? Some recent social experiments show that they can.

On Sept 18th, 2009, nine days before the Germany's general election, a youth organization called the German Federal Youth conducted voting experiment called the U18 (for under 18) to determine if children voting would have an impact on the outcomes of the general election. This experiment sought to answer the question: What impact would citizens under 18 years of age have if they are given the opportunity to vote in an election? 127,208 children cast their votes at 1,000 voting stations in an impressive show of the high interest and participatory levels of children. The youngest voter was nine years old. The results speak for themselves. Leaders of the political parties were impressed by the turnout. The mock vote of the children were not counted in the general election. Were they, however, the outcomes of the election would have been starkly different. The children had highly contrasting views from the older adult voter.

TABLE 3

Germany U18 experiment results

Political Party	U18 Results (%)	German general election results (%)
Social Democrats (SPD)	20.45	23.00
Green Party (Die Grune)	20.00	10.70
Christian Democrats (CDU/CSU)	19.35	33.80
Far Left (Die Linke)	10.35	11.90
Pirate Party (Die Piraten)	8.70	2.00
Liberals (FDP)	7.60	14.60
Animal Protection (Die Tierschutzpartei)	5.19	0.60
Others	8.36	3.40

(Sylvain & Reis, 2009)

Even if the voting age were dropped, there is another condition that must be met if children are to make real gains; they must turn up to vote. Unfortunately, recent research shows that the lowest voter turnout is consistently found in the young voters age bracket, ages 19 to 29; the very ones who could make the most difference to correcting the historical imbalances. In the 2014 US midterm elections, only 19.9% of Americans in that age bracket actually turned up to vote (Circle, 2014 Youth Turnout and Youth Registration Rates Lowest Ever Recorded; Changes Essential in 2016). This was the lowest rate of youth turnout ever recorded.

Intellectual and Political Capacity

Critics commonly argue that children are not intellectually capable nor do they have sufficient life experience to appreciate the consequences of their votes. This argument goes back all the way to Plato's Republic, written in approximately 380 BC, wherein Plato argues against democracy. In the Republic, Plato establishes that there are true answers as to how a state should be run. Next, he argues that these answers are not obvious and generally speaking, the general population will not have these answers. If leaders are chosen through a democratic process and there happens to be a charismatic leader who can easily manipulate them but lacks the true knowledge of how to run the state, the equally ignorant public could conceivably vote such a leader into power. In Plato's ideal republic, therefore, it is governed by the knowledgeable, the philosopher. Here we see the introduction of the concept of the Epistocrat, the person who has greater knowledge of the relevant normative political truths.

The argument for epistocracy or rule by the knowledgeable is set out in a series of four claims in David Estlund's *Democratic Authority* (Estlund, 2009) :

- There are true, procedure-independent normative standards by which political decisions ought to be judged. (The truth claim)

- For any demos, it is true that there is a small group of people – the epistocrats – who know those normative standards better than others and, thus, know better what the decisions that conform to those standards are. (The privileged knowledge status claim) 2

- For any demos, if it is true that the epistocrats know those standards better than others etc., then these people should have political authority over others. (The authority claim) 3

- Thus, for any given demos, epistocrats should have political authority over others. (The epistocratic conclusion)

In this classic work on Democratic theory, Estlund presents a theory called *epistemic proceduralism* which avoids epistocracy by arguing that while a few people probably do know best, this can only be used in political justification if their expertise is acceptable from all reasonable points of view.

These critics hold that children, lacking this maturity could actually damage the voting process, bringing about undesirable results. Numerous research studies show that it is not possible to broadly label everyone under 18 years of age in the same categories. Children's parliaments around the globe have achieved positive political outcomes comparable to adult parliaments (see Children's Parliament section below). In many cases, studies have shown that young teens have far more knowledge of current trends about the world, especially technological and social media than their parents.

Taxation without representation

By issuing debt of any kind, whether financial, ecological or both, this is a form of taxing the future generation (Aoki and Vaithianathan, 2009). It leaves the future generation to deal with the deficiencies in capital or the natural environment. The debt is performed by this generation without any consultation with the next generation. In other words, the youth have no political representation and in effect, this becomes a form of taxation without representation, which was one of the principles behind the American revolution.

Arguments for and Against Demeny Voting

The debate surrounding Demeny voting is very complex. Some critics argue that Demeny voting that gives parents additional votes can be easily abused. Some critics have pointed out that some cultural and religious groupings have a much higher number of children on average and they could use those votes to bias their own political agendas. Japanese researcher Reiko Aoki offers a contrasting view. When interviewed about the fairness of giving parents an additional vote, he replied that

"Currently, the pension system (the relationship between premium and receipt) is independent of how many children the person has. With pay as you go, pensions are paid by the current generation. Even if you did not spend time changing diapers, helping them learn to read and write, driving them to piano and soccer lessons, losing sleep or having to stay home when children get sick, you are paid the same amount as those who did. Is this fair?" (Sharp, 2011)

Evidence supporting Children's Political Maturity

Consider the case of children's parliaments. In a 2014 paper on the subject (Wall, 2014), researcher John Wall counted at least 30 countries which have some form of children's parliaments including: India, Norway, Germany, Slovenia, Bolivia, Ecuador, Brazil, Nigeria, Congo, Burkina Faso, Liberia, New Zealand, England, Scotland, and a Children's United Parliament of the World (Austin, 2010; Cabannes, 2005; Children's United Parliament of the World, 2009; Conrad, 2009). Some of these parliaments have made responsible decisions equal in skill, finesse, understanding and discretion to that of any adult politician (Wall, 2014). In the 1990s, one of the first children's parliaments in Rajasthan, India comprised of 6 to 14 year olds had significant positive impact on their community such as improving educational policies, dismissing poor teachers, improving community services and funding new utilities (Bajpai, 2003: 469; John, 2003: 235–9). In Bolivia, the children's parliament worked closely with the adult national assembly making important key recommendations (Sarkar and Mendoza, 2005) and in 1998, the children's parliament in Barra Mansa state, Brazil participated in the allocation of municipal funds, ensuring the city council addressed children's needs (Cabannes, 2005:1 191). In another case in Brazil, three students presented a proposal to a plenary session of Brazil's Chamber of Deputies arguing about the hazards of using flatbed trucks to transport school children. This argument was accepted by Congress (UNICEF, 2009). These cases illustrate that children are capable of making responsible decisions that impact public policy.

Progressive governments around the world are enhancing governance by giving children a voice in setting policies. In 2011, UNICEF's Inter-Parliamentary Union issued *A Handbook on Child Participation in Parliament*. This book provided governments with guidelines on how to include children in the decision making process. Successful children's participatory engagements in parliament including

- 2001- New Zealand developed an Agenda for Children based on an ambitious national consultative process in which children were asked to express their society-wide problems and desires (Brown and McCormack, 2005)

- 2003, South Africa launched the Children in Action (Dikwankwetla) project to include children in some parliamentary hearings and public debates (Jamieson and Mukoma, 2010)

- The Israeli Knesset now regularly invites children to participate in its child-related committees (Ben-Arieh and Boyer, 2005: 50)

- The government of Rwanda holds a National Summit for Children and Youth every year around a particular theme (Pells, 2010)

- 2004, the UK has instituted four Children's Commissioners (for England, Scotland, Wales and Northern Ireland), whose purpose is to promote children's concerns in government legislation and policy (Williams and Croke, 2008: 184-7)

- 2009, the Kazakstan government worked with UNICEF to organize a political consultative process with youth aged 10–24, called the National Adolescents and Youth Forum (Karkara and Khudaibergenov, 2009)

These and many more cases demonstrate the significant contributions that children can make to democratic society.

Evidence supporting Children's Lack of Political Maturity

The UN Convention for the Rights of the Child

Three years after Demeny's proposal, the UN Convention for the Rights of the Child was ratified in 1989, conferring inalienable rights to children including

Article 12

- *States Parties shall assure to the child who is capable of forming his or her own views the right to express those views freely in all matters affecting the child, the views of the child being given due weight in accordance with the age and maturity of the child.*

- *For this purpose, the child shall in particular be provided the opportunity to be heard in any judicial and administrative proceedings affecting the child, either directly, or through a representative or an appropriate body, in a manner consistent with the procedural rules of national law. (UN Human Rights, 1989)*

Article 13

- The child shall have the right to freedom of expression; this right shall include freedom to seek, receive and impart information and ideas of all kinds, regardless of frontiers, either orally, in writing or in print, in the form of art, or through any other media of the child's choice.

- The exercise of this right may be subject to certain restrictions, but these shall only be such as are provided by law and are necessary: (a) For respect of the rights or reputations of others; or (b) For the protection of national security or of public order, or of public health or morals.

Article 15

States Parties recognize the rights of the child to freedom of association and to freedom of peaceful assembly. No restrictions may be placed on the exercise of these rights other than those imposed in conformity with the law and which are necessary in a democratic society in the interests of national security or public safety, public order, the protection of public health or morals or the protection of the rights and freedoms of others.

Article 12 is a substantive right which entitles children to be active participants in their own lives, including active parts of those decisions that affect them. This should not be misconstrued; it does not mean they can run roughshod over the rights of their parents.

While the "right" belongs to the right holder, the children in this case, the "duty" is the responsibility of an agent, the state who must uphold the right for the right holder.

Together, Article 12, 13 , 15 and a few other key civil rights implies participation, even though that word is never explicitly spelled out in the document. And exactly what does participation mean? It means the ability for children to freely express their views and to take these views seriously.

Curiously, while 193 countries ratified this convention, two countries abstained, Somalia and the United States.

While Article 12 guarantees children the right to express their views in matters affecting the child, the gap between theory and reality is large. In 2009, there were 2.2 billion children under the age of 18. Only a fraction of them, those aged 16 years on if they lived in Brazil, Cuba, Indonesia or Nicuragua had voting rights (Tremmel, 2009). While the Convention serves as an important framework for any future work, there is a long way to go to ensure equity for children's rights.

In 1986, demographer Paul Demeny wrote a passing commentary in a paper exploring ways to improve low fertility rates in countries around the world (Demeny, 1986). Developed countries face a double threat of low fertility rates and an increasing proportion of elderly. These two factors exasperate the workload on the dwindling number of capable workers who need to support a growing population of the elderly. In a disproportionately older population, voting is skewed towards the needs of the elderly. One way to begin to correct this result is to increase the number of young voters by dropping the voting age. Another way is to do what Paul Demeny proposed in his paper, giving parents a proxy vote for their children. Demeny reasoned that such a proxy vote would support more policies that support the rights of children. Demeny held that children should not be in a position of having no voice for the first 18 years of their lives and suggested allowing parents to exercise their voting rights until they come of age (Demeny, 1986). In effect, Demeny envisioned a proxy vote in which each parent would receive and exercise an additional half vote for each child under his or her guardianship . Demeny's proposal gained traction in the academic and political science community and has since come to be popularly known as *Demeny voting*.

The idea of children having the basic right to vote is still a foreign concept to most people. Children's suffrage has, however, been seriously debated in Germany since 1910 and in France since 1920, where it was almost passed by the French National Assembly in the Parent's Vote issue before the assembly.

In recent years, a number of attempts have been made to grant children voting rights through Demeny voting. Two cases stand out in particular, Germany and Japan. In 2003 and again in 2008, members of the German parliament introduced the "Kinderwahlrecht" bill (German term for Demeny voting) to the Bundestag, the legislative body of the German government which would have given proxy voting rights to parents (Weimann, 2002) both the 2003 and 2008 proposals were defeated. Researcher

Udo Hermann continued investigating children's right to vote in his PhD thesis, *Economic analysis of voting rights for children* (Hermann, 2011) which explored taking the research into an economic direction.

Japan was motivated to seriously consider introducing Demeny voting for the same reasons that the United States and Germany have been exploring it; all three countries have a common problem of an increasingly older population and a shrinking youth population due to low fertility rates. Due to a lack of representation from children, policies trends in all three countries have been significantly skewed to favor the elderly and disadvantage the young. Noticing this, researchers Reiko Aoki of the Centre for Intergenerational Studies at Hitotsubashi University and Rhema Vaithianathan of the University of Auckland authored a research paper that proposed Demeny voting as a solution for low fertility rates in Japan (Aoki & Vaithianathan, 2009). Citing Japan's 2005 census, the researchers found that within the existing population, the share of the vote was skewed towards those over 55 years of age and that a Demeny vote would rebalance the share of the vote between the elderly and the young.

TABLE 3

Currently, there is no demeny voting in Japan.

	Parents of children under 18 yrs	55 yr or older
Regular voting	24%	43%
If demeny allowed	37%	35%
Net % change with Demeny	+13	- 8

(source: Aoki & Vaithianathan, 2009)

In a 2011 interview with CBC Radio, Demeny reiterated his position stating that extending rights to children was a natural progression of the democratic project and that there should no bias against generational status.

Indeed the knowledge and experience gap argument may only apply to the youngest of children, newborns and toddlers.

But even in these cases, there is growing sympathy that even they be granted rights in specific circumstances. In recent years, children and youth, organizing with sympathetic adults have launched lawsuits against various levels of governments, claiming that their inaction on climate change issues is endangering their future world. Courts have begun to agree with them, granting them a space to hear their arguments.

In the same manner that there are government policies that transfer economic resources to parents for the benefit of children, so too, it is argued there should be similar policies that transfer political resources to them.

In July 2015, a group of youth advised by Andrea Rodgers of the Western Environmental Law Center and an attorney for the teen petitioners called the decision a "landmark ruling."

In 2015, another group of youth sued the state of Oregon.

On August 12, 2015, Our Children's Trust, the group behind many of the lawsuits, filed a lawsuit against the Federal government. Their argument is that the federal government is infringing on the constitutional rights of America's youth and future generations by allowing fossil fuel extraction and consumption to continue unimpeded. The claim states that these activities cause climate change by damaging the atmosphere, and the atmosphere is a public trust, they say, that should be protected for future generations. Ultimately, they argue that this pollution discriminates against young people, who will suffer the impact of climate change far more than today's policymakers.

Mary Christina Wood, the Philip H. Knight Professor of Law
at the University of Oregon. "The fact is we have only three
branches of government. So from a lawyer's perspective, you
have to look at the structure we have and ask which part is
functional and which part of it has become corrupted through
big industry money.

"Two of the branches have become essentially corrupted
because of the campaign contributions to those two branches
of government. And so the third branch — while it's not perfect,
by any means — the federal judiciary is as close to insulated
from that big money influence as you can get."

References

Aoki, R., & Vaithianathan, R. (2009). *Is Demeny Voting the Answer to Low Fertility in Japan?* Hitosubashi: Institute of Economic Research, Hitotsubashi University.

Demeny, P. (1986). Pronatalist Policies in Low-Fertility Countries: Patterns, Performance, and Prospects. *Population and Development Review*, Vol. 12 pp. 335-358.

Estlund, D. M. (2009). *Democratic Authority.* Princeto, New Jersey: Princeton University Press.

Hermann, U. (2011). Economic analysis of voting rights for children. Berlin: Freie Universitat Berlin.

Lecce, S. (2009). Should Democracy Grow up? Children and Voting Rights. *Intergenerational Justice Review*, pp. Volume 9 - Issue 4, 133-138.

Lippert-Rasmussen, K. (2011). Estlund on Epistocracy: A Critique. *Epistemic Democracy in Practice.* New Haven, Connecticut: Yale University .

Pantell, R. H., & Shannon, M. T. (2009). Improving Public Policy for Children: A Vote for Each CHild. *Intergenerational Justice Review*, pp. pp. 139-143.

Sharp, A. (2011). *Should Parents Vote for Kids?* Retrieved january 18, 2016, from The Diplomat: http://thediplomat.com/2011/01/should-parents-vote-for-kids/

Sylvain, D., & Reis, M. d. (2009). What Would Happen if Citizens Under 18 Years Old Had the Legal Right to Vote? The German U18 Project Experience. *Intergenerational Justice Review*, pp. pp. 152-153.

UN. (2015). *World Population Prospects.* New York: United Nations, Department of Economic and Social Affiairs, Population Division.

Wall, J. (2011). Can democracy represent children? Toward a politics of difference. *Childhood*, 19(1) 86-100.

Wall, J. (2014). Why children and Youth Should Have the Right to Vote: An Argument for Proxy-CLaim Suffrage. *Children, Youth and Environments* , 24(1) 108-123.

Weimann, M. (2002). *Wahlrecht fur Kinder - Eine Streitschrift.* Berlin: Beltz.

Two Peas in a Pod: Integrating Social Capital With Delegative Democracy

A paper submitted to the Nemalux Democracy Project on April 24, 2016.

Introduction

Social capital has captured the imagination of many who conceive of a more perfect democratic reality. Similar to social capital, delegative democracy seeks to widen participation in processes that are beneficial for wide swaths of people. Added to this hopeful mix is the sobering reality that significant portions of those who comprise civil society in Western political jurisdictions have chosen to jettison their involvement with associations, organizations, and political institutions. This paper promulgates the notion that social capital and delegative democracy share conceptual and operational imperatives that taken together, can advance the cause of democracy.

The initial portion looks at the democratic implications wrought by social capital by examining definitional origins and challenges and its possibilities as a measuring stick for participatory democracy. The relationship between the individual and society is then excavated. Next, a brief comparison of social capital and the social contract is offered, followed by an exploration of some of the deleterious ramifications that arise when there is an absence of social capital.

The middle section of the paper more fully captures social capital's relationship with delegative democracy. More specifically, social capital's political-power component is interrogated within the context of delegative democracy. Portions of this segment also touch on proxy voting as a way of engaging the disengaged through expanding the pool of potential delegates, social capital's potential in reducing poverty, and interpersonal trust juxtaposed between the two concepts.

The final part of the paper is dedicated to imagining a viable way of addressing the all important task of selecting delegates within a social capital context. Accordingly, a value ranking that draws from social capital and delegative democratic conceptions provides a guideline for non-delegates to select whom they would ideally wish to transfer their vote. In so doing, a basis for giving the concept of social capital to advance democratic participation is given proverbial wings.

Social Capital and Its Democratic Implications

Though most popularized through the seminal work of Robert Putnam, a political scientist, the concept of social capital has not been monopolized by that particular field. Many disciplines claim the concept as their own. Regardless of the saliency of these claims, the term is steeped in resonance because of the need of social scientists and others to explain trends in civic engagement. For those who care about democracy, its current state or prospects for future improvement, social capital has become a touchstone because of its implications for citizen involvement both inside and outside political institutions.

According to Putnam, in its most idealized form, heightened social capital can and must produce increased civic literary. For example, instantaneous digital communication must not become a substitute for face-to-face interaction but instead increase it. Community must be restored with more congenial workplaces arising. A host of other outcomes must emerge if social capital's potential is to be realized. Acutely ambitious, this concept must not just be relegated to a discussion point for academics, but also extend to the general populous so as to become the transformational device it purports to be.

It is the promise of social capital, rather than the present reality, which captivates the minds of its contemporary proponents. Isolating one definition that encapsulates this potential is problematical because the very origins of the term are contentious. Some scholars attribute the dawning of social capital to the Middle Ages. In the modern epoch, Lyda Hanifan asserted that social capital produced certifiable assets that enhanced the daily lives of people. Goodwill, fellowship, sympathy, and social intercourse that make up social units are to be counted as contributing to social capital.[1] Note the behavioural emphasis that seems to militate against, or at the very least, de-emphasize social capital's transformative potential. Under this guise, social capital is largely a construct that seems politically innocuous and tame.

Sociologists have been prone to give at least cursory acknowledgement that social capital may encompass both present conditions and future possibilities. Pierre Bourdieu's characterization of the term as "the aggregate of the actual or potential resources which are linked to possession of a durable network of more or less institutionalized relationships of mutual acquaintance or recognition"[2] speaks to this. Bourdieu's definition tends to stress networks over cause and effect and does not really encapsulate even a passing reference to individuals. As such, its chief limitation lies in the notion that it may not be readily transferable to an action plan capable of transforming democracy.

Putnam himself stresses the collective benefits in social capital and highlights social cohesion by stating the term consists of "features of social organization, such as networks, norms

---

1   The Organization for Economic Co-operation and Development (OECD), *Human Capital: How What You Know Can Shape Your Life*, 2007. Found at: https://www.oecd.org/insights/37966934.pdf Pg. 102.

2   Alejandro Portes, "Social Capital: Its Origins and Applications in Modern Sociology," in E.L. Lesser, ed, *Knowledge and Social Capital: Foundations and Applications* (Boston: Butterworth Heinemann, 2000). Pg. 45.

and trust, that facilitate coordination and cooperation for mutual benefit…"[3] What makes Putnam's conceptualization of the term exceptional is that he dared to give social capital saliency by making it operational with an array of prescriptive measures that would ostensibly address deficiencies in a political culture that was infused with low participation. It is this linear relationship from the theoretical to the empirical that made his writings so appealing to many.

Aside from occasional oblique and rare direct remarks from political elites that wish to place severe limitations on citizen participation in decision-making processes, most practitioners in modern politics pay at least passing rhetorical homage to the merits of participatory democracy. Just what constitutes the proper amount of participation and the line between what is desirable and what is possible are highly contentious topics. Regardless of the foregoing, "participatory democrats consider breaking down apathy and maximizing active citizen engagement a main task of democrats…participatory democrats applaud the forging of solidarity as a principal virtue of democracy."[4] It is this aspiration of solidarity (or cohesion) with citizen engagement that best intersects with social capital.

One could easily interpret these two concepts as being co-dependent. After all, it is difficult to conceive of solidarity and common cause without operational networks or associations rooted in community. Similarly, upping the possibility that mutually beneficial social networks arise seems a faint hope unless genuine attempts at citizen engagement occur within communities and political jurisdictions. Research has been done that finds social capital, as manifested in associations that people make with one another, and democracy are intertwined.[5]

---

3   Robert D. Putnam, "The Prosperous Community: Social Capital and Public Life," *The American Prospect* 13 (1993): pgs. 35 & 36.

4   Frank Cunningham, *Theories of Democracy: A Critical Introduction* (London: Routledge, 2002). Pg. 123.

5   Pamela Paxton, "Social Capital and Democracy: An Interdependent Relationship," *American Sociological Review* 67, 2 (2002): pg. 255.

If participatory democracy is the aim, then social capital is a useful explanatory device and a potential measuring stick as to how the "grand project" is succeeding (or not). Populations that are disengaged from each other, socially and politically, are unlikely to have the wherewithal to meet serious challenges as they emerge. Attaining adequate levels of civic literacy, whereby citizens can make informed decisions, seems impossible without social capital's implied adult education element. Moreover, local governance may be enhanced and citizen participation broadened where social capital is prevalent.[6] The element of potentially enhanced trust is not incidental to this discussion because there is a claim that social and political trust "improves the possibilities of social cooperation, while at the same time reducing the risks of free-riding citizens and exploitative elites."[7] Trust, a main component of social capital, helps to set the stage for participation, assuring greater functionality for democratic decision-making.

As first blush, the relationship between social capital and individuals might seem superfluous or incidental. After all, the saliency of social capital hinges on notions of associations and networks rather than the classic 'every man is an island unto himself' credo. Putnam was particularly adamant that technology be used to facilitate in-person contact rather than the classical image of the lone person at their computer in a dimly-lighted room version of social networking. Some have taken to posit that in fact what has transpired is the polar opposite of Putnam's intent: online networks roughly resemble in-person communities.[8] The idea of improving interaction to the point where civic literacy is enhanced so that people can make informed political choices, very much depends on collective activities. Information can be

---

6   Sophie Body-Gendrot and Marilyn Gittell, "Introduction: Empowering Citizens: From Social Citizenship to Social Capital," in S. Body-Gendrot and M. Gittell, eds, *Social Capital and Social Citizenship* (Oxford: Lexington Books, 2002). Pg. xv.

7   Kenneth Newton, "Trust, Social Capital, Civic Society, and Democracy," *International Political Science Association* 22, 2 (2001): pg. 205.

8   Anna-Liisa Syranen and Kari Kuutti, "Trust, Acceptance, and Alignment: The Role of IT in Redirecting A Community," in M. Huysman and V. Wulf, eds, *Social Capital and Information Technology* (Cambridge, Massachusetts: MIT Press, 2002). Pg. 23.

transferred electronically but real human interaction depends on, and consequently the impact of increased social capital, is derived from shared in-person empirical experiences.

So what is left for individuals in this vortex of social capital run amuck? The key element of personal development may provide a clue as to how individuals are impacted. In addition to deriving greater awareness of community and political variables, individuals may relate to social capital as a way to grow interpersonally and intellectually. While it may be true that many networks and associations are finite in their ability to convey depth and understanding, the underpinnings of human interaction are present nonetheless. For example, those with introspective dispositions and personality traits are forced to contemplate the need to articulate with others, if only at a cursory level. Also, being part of networks that are tied into the community enables one to develop empathy, so essential if we are able to understand others and develop larger contexts' from which to make decisions and properly evaluate community needs and realities.

Keeping the foregoing in mind, *bonding* is referred to as an aspect of social capital that is viewed negatively because of its potential to promote elitistism within groups and hoarding (of materials, relationships, etc.). In contrast, *bridging* is seen as a means of promoting the act of information dispersing and gaining access to external resources.[9] Extrapolating from this, it should be obvious that there are important democratic ramifications for the individual. The first of which is that social networking groups that error on the side of bonding may work to narrow the overall community and be deleterious in terms of promoting solutions that could address the greater (or wider) good. Concomitantly, individuals who are enmeshed with associations and networks that embody bridging characteristics come closer to realizing

---

9   Fiona M. Kay and Richard Johnston, "Ubiquity and Disciplinary Contrasts of Social Capital," in F.M. Kay and R. Johnston, eds, *Social Capital, Diversity, and the Welfare State* (Vancouver: UBC Press, 2007). Pg. 24.

the potential upside of increased social capital. The latter category furthers the aims of social cohesion because they actively work to militate against citizen disengagement. This one dynamic can determine whether individuals in a social capital framework move along democratic participation or their opposite. It's also worth noting that individuals exhibit free agency or choice as to which networks and associations they elect to involve themselves with. On that basis, there is an element of self-selection that determines the shape and potential of community networks.

Because of some similar points of emphasis there is a danger that social capital and the social contract become interchangeable in popular discourse. Arising from the age of Absolutism that coloured the thinking and societal relationships in the West during the Middle Ages and beyond, the social contract strove to redefine those relationships. Thomas Hobbes revived the ancient term by asserting that people should be guided by their own conscience, independent of the state.[10] A series of other philosophers challenged and modulated this interpretation but Jean-Jacques Rousseau made it his own with a seminal work entitled *The Social Contract*. In it, Rousseau articulated a re-thinking of the roles citizens should enjoy within society. Instead of absolute deference, those holding property were henceforth to have obligations to their fellow citizens. In fact, the term citizen took on new meaning under the social contract, inferring a claim to equal status. This trenchant exclamation point became the basis for the French Revolution, a revolution that cemented the role of the citizen in Europe.

The distance from the Hobbesian claim of natural rights to Rousseau's conception that laws are not natural but stem from the minds and actions of humans is great and it may be asserted that the latter interpretation won out. The collective creation of laws flowed from the general will. It is here the

---

10 Thomas Hobbes, *Leviathan* (London: Penguin, 1985). Pgs. 12-15.

social contract and social capital intersect for if the latter be in a state of receding, the possibility of a social contract (under some either guise or term) reduces in likelihood. Constructs such as rights and obligations can only really be imbibed by citizens through the participation of networks and associations. Even if those associations occur in a formal sense, such as a classroom, a type of bridging occurs that allows for the transmission of ideas.

Further symbiosis between the two terms announces itself under the heading *social cohesion.* As previously discovered, if people ascribe to associations and networks that serve to bridge rather than bond, social capital can carry on with the task of attempting to produce social cohesion and solidarity. "Networks also constitute communities that socialize their members to identify with other members of the community, to contribute to the group, and to impose normative constraints on their actions."[11] Rousseau maintained that the purpose of any political association was to further the well-being of its members. Consequently, the greater the numbers that comprise the organization (s) the chances are a better government will prevail.[12]

One form of interpretation would be to posit that social capital is the progressive realization of the term social contract inasmuch as it attempts to make relationships more operational. To wit: good governments are not just achieved with consent of the governed but with the participation of the governed.[13] The link between social capital and the social contract is further under-girded with the knowledge that the latter depends on the notion that citizens ought throw themselves unreservedly into associations so as to protect their individual well-being collectively.[14]

---

11 Rene Bekkers, Beate Volker, Martin van der Gaag, and Henk Flap, "Social Networks of Participants in Voluntary Associations," in N. Lin and B.H. Erickson, eds, *Social Capital: An International Research Program* (Oxford, England: Oxford University Press, 2008). Pg. 185.

12 Jean-Jacques Rousseau, *The Social Contract* viewed at: http://www.earlymoderntexts.com/assets/pdfs/rousseau1762.pdf Pg. 43.

13 Marilyn Gittell, "Participation, Social Capital, and Social Change," in S. Body-Gendrot and M. Gittell, *Social Capital and Social Citizenship* (Oxford: Lexington Books, 2002). Pg. 3.

14 Jean-Jacques Rousseau, *The Social Contract* viewed at: http://www. earlymoderntexts.com/assets/pdfs/rousseau1762.pdf Pg. 7.

It helps to know what is at stake. The absence of social capital means that people essentially retreat into their own personal activities that often exclude meaningful interact with others, limiting their personal growth and that of their communities. Beyond that, political participation is impaired and political institutions suffer because they lack they informed consent and participation that democracy insists upon.

As Putnam and countless other researchers have found, the easiest and most accessible of tasks, casting a ballot during elections, was in state of pronounced decline by the 1990s and has remained low in many Western democracies. Disengagement has meant that in addition to macro level politics suffering, the chances of resolving common community level or micro concerns has lessened. Town hall meetings, membership in a political party, membership in community organizations, have all declined, despite increased levels of education, a variable that previously indicated higher levels of civic engagement.[15]

With declining participation also comes an erosion of political cognition or civic literacy.[16] So, while citizens may have academic credentials, their ability to strengthen civil society is undercut by a lack of involvement in networks, associations, and formal and informal political processes. With the withering of social capital, the ability of society to come to grips with overarching issues dissipates. One current example is that of climate change. Public goods, such as non-threatening and predictable climate patterns, are jeopardized when collective action made easier by social capital is diminished.[17] Even successful remedial adaptation is placed in doubt when citizens retreat from social capital processes that would promote political consensus and problem-solving.

15   Robert D. Putnam, "Bowling Alone: America's Declining Social
      Capital," *Journal of Democracy* 6, 1 (1995): Pgs. 5 & 6.

16   Henry Milner, *Civic Literacy: How Informed Citizens Make Democracy Work*
      (Lebanon, New Hampshire: University of New England Press, 2002). Pgs. 3-4.

17   W. Neil Adger, "Social Capital, Collective Action, and Adaptation to
      Climate Change," *Economic Geography* 79, 4 (2003): pg. 391.

Another deleterious outcome for the absence of social capital
is the passage of long-term knowledge and practices from
one generation to another. Such a state of affairs can lead to
the repetition of mistakes and errors in terms of community
organization and public policy errors. It may also deprive
future generations of a sense of continuity and corporate
memory. Beyond that, even the family unit is affected by low
levels of social capital. If social or community relationships
between sets of parents are low, the development of life
opportunities for their children may become limited.[18]

Part Two: What does Social Capital mean for Delegative Democracy?

If delegative democracy may be seen as a format or gateway
that permits democracy to strengthen and widen itself then a
key helpmate is social capital. It seems highly improbable that
civil society would have the tools to adopt new approaches to
democracy if it did not possess the collective analytical capacity
and organizational prowess to do so. Moreover, social capital
can be viewed metaphorically as a table-setter for delegative
democracy because it helps to create the conditions by
which democracy itself can be re-imagined and re-invented.
This is separate and apart from how proponents of social
capital have come to view their position as being capable
of renewing institutions via "networks of civic morality."[19]

What the two concepts have in common is an implied
desire to construct realities in which power is diffuse rather
than concentrated. This fundamental precept is central to
understanding how social capital and delegative democracy
(also anointed liquid democracy) interact. Within that similarity
there exists a key point of departure. Whereas social capital,

---

18 James S. Coleman, "The Creation and Destruction of Social Capital: Implications for
    the Law," *Notre Dame Journal of Law, Ethics, & Public Policy* 3, 3 (1988): pg. 387.

19 Lindsay Paterson, "Civic Society and Democratic Renewal," in S. Baron, J. Field, and T. Schuller, eds, in
    Social Capital: Critical Perspectives (Oxford, England: Oxford University Press, 2000). Pg. 39.

in its operational form, aims to create an *awareness* of power
that can be harnessed for community aims and aspirations,
delegative democracy, through proxy voting, is the *utilization*
of power more directly with and within institutions.

Even those that do not acknowledge social capital, who invariably
subscribe to what is referred to as the myth of the individual,[20] have
a power relationship with others, declared or not. Regardless of
one's economic, social or political station in life, the interaction with
others triggers life opportunities that emanate from the presence
of social capital. The networking that exists within social capital
also permits a type of cognition to occur within civil society that
makes people collectively aware of their democratic options.

Choice is also at the forefront of delegative democracy.
Whether one is a delegate acting on behalf of others or
whether one confers one's proxy vote to another is dependent
on choice. Furthermore, under delegative democracy those
who are delegates or proxies do not possess a uniform
power, but instead see it as a means of acting on behalf of
others with a view to playing a more direct role in the life of
a particular institution.[21] Under this approach to democracy,
power is more diffuse yet its participants potentially enjoy a
greater say as to the conduct of the institution in question.

It is not surprising that power diffusion is a desired outcome
for proponents of both social capital and delegative
democracy. Even traditional institutions such as national
parliaments have varying forms of power sharing that affect
the political culture within their jurisdictions. This has been
known to shape the choices of the electorate, thereby partially
determining the very make-up of parliaments themselves.[22]

20 Wayne Baker, *Achieving Success Through Social Capital* (San
    Francisco, California: Jossey-Bass, 2000). Pg. 2.

21 Bryan Ford, *Delegative Democracy* viewed at: http://www.brynosaurus.
    com/log/2002/0515-DelegativeDemocracy.pdf Pg. 3.

22 Orit Keder, "How Diffusion of Power in Parliaments Affects Voter
    Choice," *Political Analysis* 13, 4 (2005): Pg. 411.

Political apathy among Western democracies has been a hallmark of the contemporary period.[23] Entire libraries worth of research have attempted to excavate the causations and nature of the disengagement that has befallen democratic societies. Could the dominance of representative democracy be on the wane? The idea of once every four or five years making a decision to elevate a representative that may or may not carry out one's wishes has decreasing appeal, especially in jurisdictions that retain the antiquated first-past-the-post voting system.

One possible remedy that could imbue political culture with an ethic of participation and control over the outcome of public policy is that of delegative democracy. Using social capital's implied capability of raising the level of civic literacy and participation, delegative democracy's chief contribution is that it could ideally expand the number of decision makers within democratic institutions. It also allows those that consider themselves less than well-versed with policies and practices to vest their trust and votes with those who are adjudged to be able to make decisions. While there is much to be established in terms of the mechanics of delegative democracy, or proxy voting, the basic rationale and impetus are in place, waiting to be made operational.

The disaffection that has been so prevalent can be traced to a variety of sources ranging from the social, political, economic and cultural. Individual political actors have largely either shrugged their shoulders or waxed eloquently about the situation (focusing on the inherent dangers to democracy) and gone about their business as if nothing were amiss. Political parties, who are at the center of most political systems,[24] invest much energy in mobilizing those who are inclined to vote for them. However, this almost exclusively occurs during elections, when so much is at stake *for them*.

---

23 Roger Scully, Richardwyn Jones, and Dafydd Trystan, "Turnout, Participation, and Legitimacy in Post-Devolution Wales," *British Journal of Political Science* 34, 3 (2004): Pg. 519.

24 Hans Daalder, "The Rise of Parties in Western Democracies," in L. Diamond and R. Gunther, eds, *Political Parties and Democracy* (Baltimore, Maryland: Johns Hopkins University Press, 2001). Pg. 40.

This election-only orientation can alienate voters and reeks of blatant opportunism. Political parties could chose to go beyond their immediate need for power and in doing so would ironically enhance their legitimacy at being in the very center of governance. To do so would require a commitment to democratic principles that often go absence in the quest for a favorable electoral outcome. More specifically, if political parties engaged citizens between elections, their credibility would grow along with democratic participation.

In a similar vein, delegative democracy could be a vehicle by which parties offered citizens a more active role in their everyday politics. While parties do have a form of proxy voting at their conventions and policy meetings, such occurrences are restricted to vote tabulations at events that happen infrequently in the political cycle. If proxy voting is to be the means by which the disengaged can be brought back into the democratic fold, political parties will likely have to be part of the solution, given their predominate position within democratic institutions. Without a degree of constancy and or regularity, proxy voting takes on the aura of a symbolic act that is unleashed when power is least at stake.

With the promise of an expansion of participants from delegative democracy's virtue of compelling institutions to adopt proxy voting as an alternative to unsatisfying representative democracy, the importance of social capital takes on urgency. In particular, the need to lessen and eliminate alienation that is borne out of poverty and economic disenfranchisement becomes paramount. For those who are consumed with the daily struggle to exist are seldom convinced that their democratic participation ought to become a high-ranking priority.

Advocates of social capital have long equated the attainment of knowledge and skills with increased economic opportunity that in turn facilitates greater democratic participation.[25] It is this

---

25 Partha Dasgupta, "Economic Progress and the Idea of Social Capital," in P. Dasgupta and I. Serageldin, eds, *Social Capital: A Multifacted Perspective* (Washington, D.C.: The World Bank, 2000). Pg. 326,

personal development credo within a community or collective vortex that gives flight to social capital's more optimistic claims, namely that it can be transformative. The most important component that ushers in this positive outcome are cross-cutting relationships that social capital produces when groups practice bridging. Researchers have found that when organizations cross-cut, economic vitality is established to groups that have been economically deprived and marginalized. Also imperative is that democratic institutions change laws and practices that enable groups and social networks to flourish and promote mobility.[26]

As market-driven boom and bust cycles have come to typify capitalist societies, economic dislocation has become pervasive. The bridging capabilities inherent in social capital militate against prolonged economic estrangement because of its capacity to create groups that advocate for poverty-stricken sub-groups and individuals within organizations and associations. Given the swirling nature of the economic winds that have come to typify post-industrial societies, to be devoid of the benefits of social capital is to be condemned to perpetual poverty.

At stake is whether we are to optimize our democratic potential. If large segments of communities are perpetually outside of the ambit of democratic processes due to their economic dislocation institutions lose their standing and legitimacy as effective producers of public policy. It is difficult to imagine conditions ripe for democratic innovation would occur if poverty persisted over the long-term. Social capital's operational imperatives, residing on the pillars of interpersonal trust through collective action via groups and associations, are vital to addressing this compelling dilemma.

Given the foregoing, it should be made explicitly clear that advocates of social capital regard their concept and application as resting on interpersonal trust. A survey of the

---

26 Deepa Naarayan, "Bonds and Bridges: Social Capital and Poverty,"
    World Bank Policy Research Paper 2167 1999. Pgs. 1 & 2.

literature on delegative democracy and proxy voting
also confirms this element as central to its own efficacy.
In a sense, interpersonal trust is the glue that may keep
social capital and delegative democracy together.

It follows that mutual obligations can only manifest
themselves if interpersonal trust is established within
groups and associations. Those obligations are often given
nothing more than rhetorical treatment but are instead
implied.[27] Without the establishment of interpersonal
trust, it is difficult, if not impossible, to imagine that
social capital could lead anywhere tangible in terms of
transforming communities. It is also apparent that trust
operates alongside interdependence within networks.
This interdependence affects the "flow of material and
non-material resources."[28] Taken in this light, interpersonal
trust supplies the pre-condition, and interdependence
provides the means, for groups and communities to
advance their interests under social capital's rubric.

Under delegative democracy, trust is wrapped up in
accountability. Transparent actions and processes ideally
serve to reinforce trust, which perpetuates the belief that
power is more diffuse, thereby producing decisions that
have greater democratic legitimacy. Bryan Ford, a chief
proponent of delegative democracy, uses the example of
open balloting. He posits that accountability and trust are
more likely to become manifest if non-secret voting occurs.[29]
From an institution-building perspective, the assumption
is that secret balloting under proxy voting could eradicate
trust and render decision-making devoid of facts and logic.
Conversely, the open-balloting by delegates promotes a

27 Tom Schuller, Stephen Baron, and John Field, "Social Capital: A Review and
    Critique," in S. Baron, J. Field, and T. Schuller, eds, *Social Capital: Critical
    Perspectives* (Oxford, England: Oxford University Press, 2000). Pg. 1.

28 Ibid. Pg. 19.

29 Bryan Ford, *Delegative Democracy* viewed at: http://www.brynosaurus.
    com/log/2002/0515-DelegativeDemocracy.pdf Pgs. 5 & 6.

more rigorous form of democracy because those vesting their trust in them can trace their votes. Also, the larger community can see the fruits of the delegative system when open voting is practiced by those entrusted with the decision-making power.

Least you get the wrong impression, the history of proxy voting has not necessarily been characterized by openness.[30] For example, political parties have held conventions in which delegates voted via secret ballot. The rationale for such an approach asserted that intimidation of delegates could pervade at events which important decisions are made. This would suggest that trust among party members is low. If interpersonal trust is high, it would seem to follow that the need for such measures would likely dissipate. Political leadership conventions in the West have largely thrown away the delegate system in favour of the one-person, one-vote formula. Nevertheless, among countries that selected party leaders by delegate format, Canada was seen as more democratic, even with secret balloting at the convention, namely because of local delegate selection processes that appeared to be more inclusive.[31] Based on the political party experience, building trust within organizations so that proxy voting could emerge as a preferred option requires it to be regularly utilized, rather than episodic.

Part Three: "Adding" to Social Capital's Entrenchment in Delegate Selection

Bringing the idea of delegative democracy to life and optimizing its ideals entails the need to transfer its conceptual impetus to a utilitarian reality. Harnessing social capital is central to this goal for reasons expounded upon earlier in this paper. It is the aspiration of this short section to intertwine

---

30 See, Burton Rothberg and Steven Lilien, "Mutual Funds and Proxy Voting: New Evidence of Corporate Governance," *Journal of Business and Technology Law* 1, 1 (2006): pg. 159. & Roberta Romano, "Does Confidential Proxy Voting Matter?" *Berkley Program in Law and Economics Working Paper Series* viewed at: http://escholarship.org/uc/item/9z88z4th (2002) Pgs. 1 & 2.

31 Ofer Kenig, "Democratization of Party Leadership Selection: Do Wider Selectorates Produce More Competitive Contests?" *Electoral Studies* 28 (2008): pg. 243.

delegative democracy with social capital in the form
of an "adder" that helps to create the means by which
these ideas can be animated in institutional settings.

Imbuing values into a method that measures social capital
within institutions needs to be undertaken because without
the values that embodies the concept[32] any project that
purports to espouse delegative democracy would be
found wanting. It has been asserted elsewhere in this paper
that democracy would be improved upon if a delegative
model of democracy based on the precepts of social
capital were to be adapted. What follows is a method by
which the concept becomes more readily accessible.

The notion of bringing more people into democratic
decision-making is a shared objective of many. The means
to achieve this rests on institutions adopting proxy voting.
Just how could this aim be accomplished after those
who have determined they wish to participate or not
participate as delegates have done so? *More specifically,
on what basis would voting delegates be chosen?*

The point of initiation is to establish what values take
precedence over others and to attribute appropriate weight
to them. Whoever embodies these values and attributes is
clearly a delegate worthy of voting transfer. One disclaimer
before embarking on a listing of criteria: in accordance with
Ford's maxim that the barrier for participation as a delegate
be kept low (otherwise the key goal of egalitarianism would be
sacrificed),[33] it is important to keep in mind that the selection
of delegates are in the hands of those who wish to transfer
their vote. Furthermore, it is desirable to ensure that some core
social capital literacy is established among non-delegates.

---

32 Wenpin Tsai and Sumantra Ghoshal, "Social Capital and Value Creation: The Role of Intrafirm
   Networks," *The Academy of Management Journal* 41, 4 (1998): pgs. 464 & 465.

33 Bryan Ford, *Delegative Democracy* viewed at: http://www.brynosaurus.com/log/2002/0515-
   DelegativeDemocracy.pdf Pg.

To aid the process along, we espouse the adder below:

Value: Trust
Weight: 50%
Rationale: This boils down to the extent and frequency
with which you would be willing to transfer your vote
to the prospective delegate. Who in the organization
is trustworthy in the context of vote transfer?

Value: Leadership qualities
Weight: 25%
Rationale: Who in the group sees bridging and
cross-cutting opportunities? Are they able to see
interdependence in a developmental light that
promotes the objective of social cohesion?

Value: Seniority and Experience
Weight: 10%
Rationale: Such a person is able to promote common
purpose and have longer term knowledge, thereby allowing
the group to contextualize events, access to resources, etc.

Value: Civic Engagement
Weight: 5-10%
Rationale: The person has the capacity to
understand the need to engage both within
and without the group or organization.

As can be adduced, value features of social capital
and delegative democracy have been interspersed in
the above adder. By doing so, delegate selection can
reside within the conceptual framework of social capital.
This does not mean that other pertinent values may
not influence the determination of what constitutes
a competent delegate and becomes the criteria by
which a selection is made. Instead, it is offered as a
guidepost that enables non-delegates the ability to
choose a delegate within a social capital context.

The imperative of the adder is that it provides the framework by which delegates can be selected while at the same time promoting a diverse array of people that will be able to participate. This latter point is brought home thanks to the low qualification threshold, in combination with the requisite values referenced with delegate selection. While the adder is not a cure-all, it can be used as a direct link to the values that make social capital and delegative democracy attractive. Trust, leadership, leadership qualities, empirical experience, and civic engagement all fall comfortably within the profile of people who are able to make informed democratic decisions. Bridging from one group to another, they possess the cognition skills to function as delegates. For those who do not imagine themselves as delegates in the immediate sense, the sharing of information and resources enables them to enhance their core competencies and civic literacy, permitting them the choice of switching to eventual delegate status should they desire.

Conclusion

This paper has proved that the conceptual linkage between social capital and delegative democracy is conducive to the advancement of democratic participation. The intersection of the two terms and their complimentary applications, make for operational possibilities that are tantalizing. The initial section was concerned with social capital and its implications. The second portion of this paper illuminated the connections between social capital and delegative democracy, while the last element articulated a framework for non-delegates to select their proxies while being grounded in a social capital value system. The ongoing project to improve democracy will rightly consume more alteration and re-invention because of its power to capture the popular spirit and imagination of people everywhere.

Bibliography

Adger, W. Neil. "Social Capital, Collective Action, and Adaptation to Climate Change." *Economic Geography.* 79, 4 (2003): 387-404.

Baker, Wayne. *Achieving Success Through Social Capital.* San Francisco, California: Jossey-Bass, 2000.

Bekkers, Rene, Volker, Beate, van der Gaag, Martin, and Henk Flap. "Social Networks of Participants in Voluntary Associations." *Social Capital: An International Research Program.* Eds. N. Lin and B.H. Erickson. Oxford, England: Oxford University Press, 2008. 185-205.

Body-Gendrot, Sophie, and Gittell, Marilyn. "Introduction: Empowering Citizens: From Social Citizenship to Social Capital" *Social Capital and Social Citizenship.* Eds. S. Body-Gendrot and M. Gittell. Oxford: Lexington Books, 2002. ix-xvi.

Coleman, James S. "The Creation and Destruction of Social Capital: Implications for the Law." *Notre Dame Journal of Law, Ethics, & Public Policy.* 3, 3 (1988): 375-404.

Cunningham, Frank. *Theories of Democracy: A Critical Introduction.* London: Routledge, 2002.

Daalder, Hans. "The Rise of Parties in Western Democracies." *Political Parties and Democracy.* Eds. L. Diamond and R. Gunther. Baltimore, Maryland: Johns Hopkins University Press, 2001. 40-51.

Dasgupta, Partha. "Economic Progress and the Idea of Social Capital." *Social Capital: A Multifacted Perspective.* Eds.

P. Dasgupta and I. Serageldin. Washington, D.C.: The World Bank, 2000. 325-424.

Ford, Bryan. *Delegative Democracy.* (2002) viewed at: http://www.brynosaurus.com/log/2002/0515-DelegativeDemocracy.pdf

Gittell, Marilyn. "Participation, Social Capital, and Social Change." *Social Capital and Social Citizenship.* Eds. S. Body-Gendrot and M. Gittell. Oxford: Lexington Books, 2002. 3-12.

Hobbes, Thomas. *Leviathan.* London: Penguin, 1985.

Kay, Fiona M., and Johnston, Richard. "Ubiquity and Disciplinary Contrasts of Social Capital." *Social Capital, Diversity, and the Welfare State.* Eds. F.M. Kay and R. Johnston. Vancouver: UBC Press, 2007.

Keder, Orit. "How Diffusion of Power in Parliaments Affects Voter Choice." *Political Analysis.* 13, 4 (2005): 410-429.

Kenig, Ofer. "Democratization of Party Leadership Selection: Do Wider Selectorates Produce More Competitive Contests?" *Electoral Studies.* 28 (2008): 240-247.

Milner, Henry. *Civic Literacy: How Informed Citizens Make Democracy Work.* Lebanon, New Hampshire: University of New England Press, 2002.

Naarayan, Deepa. "Bonds and Bridges: Social Capital and Poverty." *World Bank Policy Research Paper 2167.* 1999.

Newton, Kenneth. "Trust, Social

Capital, Civic Society, and Democracy." *International Political Science Association.* 22, 2 (2001): 201-214.

The Organization for Economic Co-operation and Development (OECD). *Human Capital: How What You Know Can Shape Your Life.* 2007. Found at: https://www.oecd.org/insights/37966934.pdf

Paterson, Lindsay. "Civic Society and Democratic Renewal." *Social Capital: Critical Perspectives.* Eds. S. Baron, J. Field, and T. Schuller. Oxford, England: Oxford University Press, 2000. 39-55.

Paxton, Pamela. "Social Capital and Democracy: An Interdependent Relationship." *American Sociological Review.* 67, 2 (2002): 254-277.

Portes, Alejandro. "Social Capital: Its Origins and Applications in Modern Sociology." *Knowledge and Social Capital: Foundations and Applications.* Ed. E.L. Lesser. Boston: Butterworth Heinemann, 2000. 43-67.

Putnam, Robert. D. "Bowling Alone: America's Declining Social Capital." *Journal of Democracy.* 6, 1 (1995): 65-78.

Putnam, Robert D. "The Prosperous Community: Social Capital and Public Life." *The American Prospect.* 13 (1993): 35-42.

Romano, Roberta. "Does Confidential Proxy Voting Matter?" *Berkley Program in Law and Economics Working Paper Series.* (2002): viewed at: http://escholarship.org/uc/item/9z88z4th

Rothberg, Burton, and Lilien, Steven. "Mutual Funds and Proxy Voting: New Evidence of Corporate Governance." *Journal of Business and Technology Law.* 1, 1 (2006): 157-184.

Rousseau, Jean-Jacques. *The Social Contract.* 1762. viewed at: http://www.earlymoderntexts.com/assets/pdfs/rousseau1762.pdf

Schuller, Tom, Baron, Stephen, and Field, John. "Social Capital: A Review and Critique." *Social Capital: Critical Perspectives.* Eds. S. Baron, J. Field, and T. Schuller. Oxford, England: Oxford University Press, 2000. 1-38.

Scully, Roger, Jones, Richardwyn, and Trystan, Dafydd. "Turnout, Participation, and Legitimacy in Post-Devolution Wales." *British Journal of Political Science.* 34, 3 (2004): 519-537.

Syranen, Anna-Liisa, and Kuutti, Kari. "Trust, Acceptance, and Alignment: The Role of IT in Redirecting A Community." *Social Capital and Information Technology.* Eds. M. Huysman and V. Wulf. Cambridge, Massachusetts: MIT Press, 2002.

Tsai, Wenpin, and Ghoshal, Sumantra. "Social Capital and Value Creation: The Role of Intrafirm Networks." *The Academy of Management Journal.* 41, 4 (1998): 464-476.

Simulation of Proxy Voting for Expertise-Based Decisions

Geometric Energy Corporation
June 30, 2016

Execute summary

Following a mathematical analysis of proxy voting as an alternative to direct democracy, a simulation study was performed to obtain optimistic benchmarks for proxy-voting outcomes. The latter has allowed us to determine that, under the model assumptions, proxy voting increases the likelihood of the optimal outcome over democracy. The extent of this effect is mediated by the trust threshold. At an 60%, 80 and 95% trust threshold we see a breakpoint of ~85%, ~75%, and ~55% expertise, respectively, whereas in democracy we see a breakpoint of 50%. Introducing a simple model for the Dunning-Kruger effect negatively influences the expected outcomes. The 60%, 80% and 95% trust threshold have their breakpoints drop to ~55%, ~52%, and ~50% respectively. Introducing considerations of realism for the trust threshold parameter indicates a priori that it is likely that proxy-voting is not much better than democracy, especially in presence of the Dunning-Kruger effect. Consequently, proxy voting is recommended against until psychological effects can be better guarded against.

Methods

This is a simulation of the model described in 'Mathematical modelling of proxy voting'. The code for the simulation was implemented in the R-language and is present in its entirety in the Code Appendix section. The number of voters was kept at 100 for all runs and all the vote-transfer weights were set to '1'. The number of runs for each parameter setting was fixed at 1000. The metric used to compare the two voting models was probability of the optimal decision attaining absolute majority in an election. The level of expertise at which this probability is 50% is termed the 'breakpoint'.

Before continuing a point should be noted about interpreting the trust threshold parameter. If two voters A and B have a (directed) connection, then that connection has a trust value. Lets say A –> B (A trusts B – to some extent). The trust threshold is how much you need to trust somebody before you can transfer your vote to them. Now, the trust threshold relates to a larger property about connections globally - percentage of vote-transfer-trustworthy connections. Because the trust values are randomly assigned, only a fraction of those connections are going to effectively be relevant to proxy voting. Consequently if the trust threshold is 80%, only 20% of all connections are going to be relevant and at the individual level you see that as an average of 1/5 connections being trustworthy. In addition, it is also worth noting that in these models the decision to transfer a vote is compulsory. When the trust threshold and expertise (i.e. larger reported expertise of proxy-voter) conditions are met a vote must be transferred. Therefore we ought to be wary of extrapolation to political settings where a vote might be kept regardless of these conditions being met.

Results & Analysis

The simulations performed in this study seem indicative of the clear superiority of proxy voting (see Figures 1-3 in the Figure Appendix section). When the trust threshold is 60% and the Dunning-Kruger effect is absent we find that the population attains voting majority with a breakpoint of ~85% (see Figure 1) and fairly reliably for expertise thresholds no larger than ~75%. Similarly, we find that at an 80 and 95% trust threshold we see a breakpoint of ~75%, and ~55% expertise, respectively, whereas in democracy we see a breakpoint of 50%. These graphs depict the intuition that on a matter requiring solely subject-matter expertise democracy is a poor choice for deciding on the best course of action.

The Dunning-Kruger (DK) effect is a cognitive bias by means of which an individual perceives their skill with a bias that is negatively proportional to their skill (e.g. the unskilled believe themselves experts and experts believe themselves unskilled). This has the effect of making the unskilled keep their vote more often than they should - possibly getting more votes – and making the experts relinquish their votes more often than they should.

The importance of the DK effect comes into the model as a critique of expertise perception of the self and of others. If expertise is objectively measurable, the DK effect is rendered a moot point. However, if it isn't objectively measurable then self-reporting systems need to be utilized and it is here that the DK effect enters the model. Depending on the specific relationship that this takes in the voting population, the effects may be more or less dramatic. In particular in this study, the function modeling the DK effect has been chosen to be determined by $perceivedExpertise = f(actualExpertise)$ where $f(x) = \lambda \sin(2\pi x)/(2\pi) + x$ and λ is a free parameter that is larger the larger the DK effect is. The choice of this function is motivated by its shape that is a line of unit slope overlayed with a hump for lower values of x (i.e. models positive bias for low expertise) and a valley for higher values of x (i.e. models negative bias for high levels of expertise). In these simulations the parameter λ has been set to 2, as opposed to 0, when the DK effect is present.

In figures 4-6 we see how the DK-effect has effectively diminished to some extent the reliability of the proxy voting outcomes. Though the breakpoints have dropped significantly, all of them being between 50% and 55%. However we still see that the right tail of the curve of proxy-voting is appreciably above that of democracy. However, the important point to be made is how strong the influence of the DK effect can be.

Limitations

Though the results look promising, let's analyze the parameter values. A 60% trust threshold is an unrealistic value - it entails that (on average) 40% of all connections are trustworthy enough for you to pass them your vote. Similarly, 80% seems a little unrealistic. The 95% trust threshold is more likely in a real world setting. However, at 95% trust threshold the Dunning-Kruger effect can be significant enough to weaken the small advantages that exist for proxy voting, with results not significantly better than democracy. Of course, the precise magnitude of the effect is going to depends on a more accurate DK model.

Another point to consider is that it's possible that in more realistic social networks the negative effects of DK could be further amplified. In a very connected network, vote transfers can propagate very far in the network as opposed to a fairly disconnected one. A more thorough analysis of the proxy voting model should attempt to understand the relationship between network connectivity and the influence of the DK effect.

Conclusion

The simulation study carried out to estimate grossly the potential benefits of proxy voting indicate that proxy voting has its benefits. If proxy voting is effectively a deferral to experts and that deferral is based on objective expertise differences, proxy voting can be superior to democracy on an expertise-related decision making issue. However, if expertise differences are measured subjectively (e.g. self reporting) psychological effects like Dunning-Kruger garnish most of the benefits of proxy voting, the extent of which is suspected to depend strongly on the social structure of the voting populace. A simulation study to that end seems feasible. As a result of these observations, proxy voting is recommended against until psychological barriers to accurate deferral can be mitigated.

createPlot(simulationResults_60_0,"Fig 1. Proxy voting: 60% trust threshold & No DK effect")

FIG 1
Proxy voting: 60% trust threshold & No DK effect

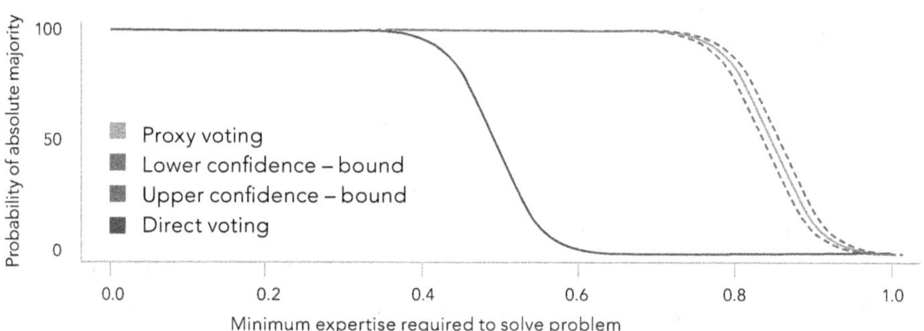

createPlot(simulationResults_80_0,"Fig 2. Proxy voting: 80% trust threshold & No DK effect")

FIG 2
Proxy voting: 80% trust threshold & No DK effect

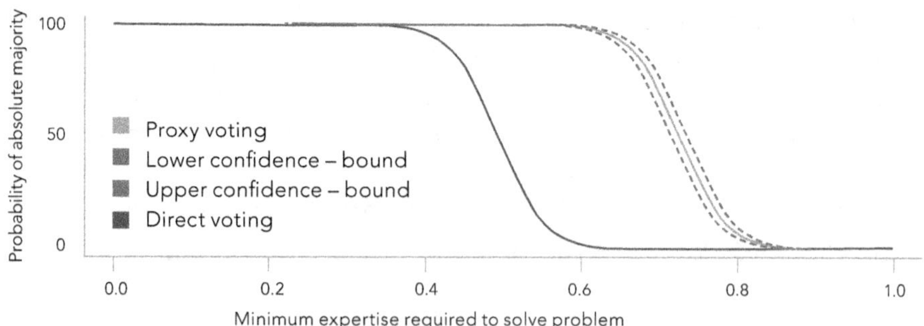

createPlot(simulationResults_95_0,"Fig 3. Proxy voting: 95% trust
threshold & No DK effect")

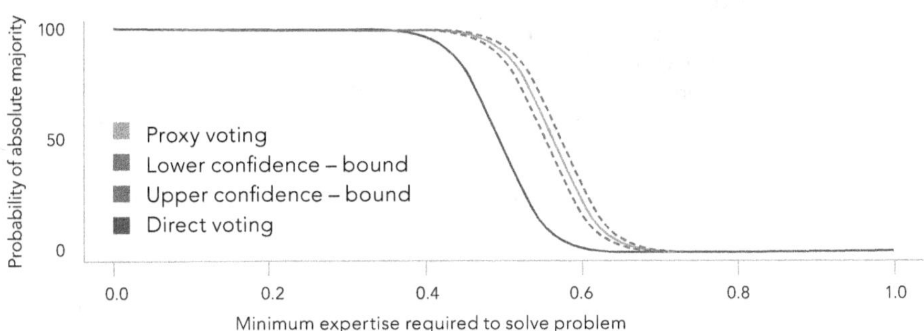

Effect of Dunning-Kruger
createPlot(simulationResults_60_2,"Fig 4. Proxy voting: 60% trust
threshold & DK effect")

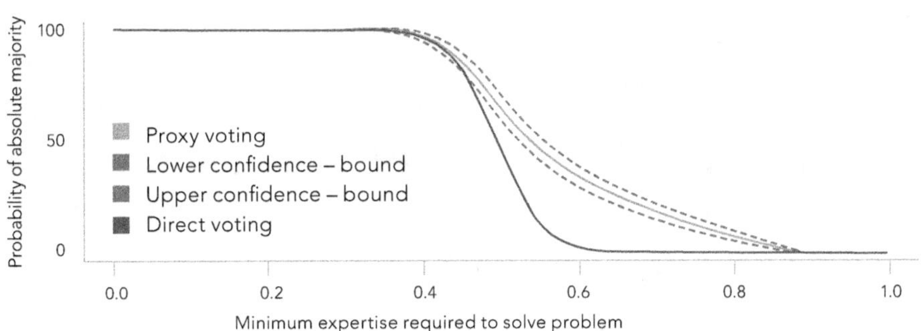

createPlot(simulationResults_80_2,"Fig 5. Proxy voting: 80% trust threshold & DK effect")

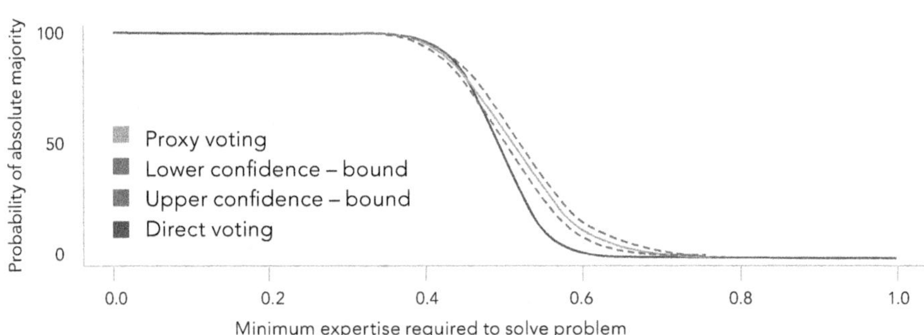

createPlot(simulationResults_95_2,"Fig 6. Proxy voting: 95% trust threshold & DK effect")

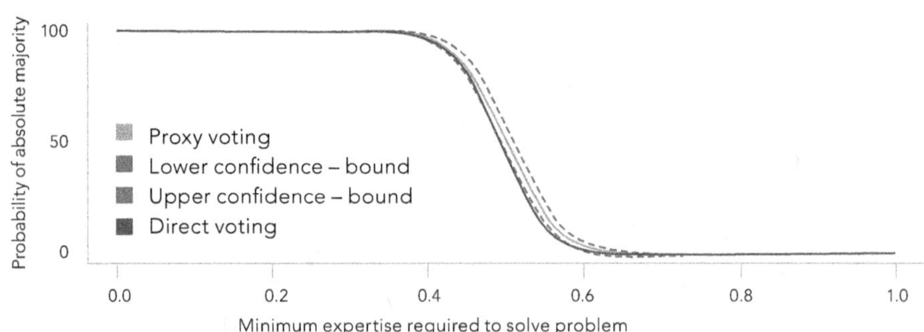

Coding Appendix

```r
library(expm)
set.seed(1426) #Set random seed for testing purposes
num_participants <- 100 #Population size
numberOfExpertiseLevels <- 1001 #Number of expertise levels to use
in the plotting stage
minimumconfidence <- .6 #i.e. Minimum trust to be given a vote
minimumExpertise <- seq(0,1,length.out=numberOfExpertiseLevels)
DK_SkewParameter <- 0

dunningKrugerEffect <- function(actualExpertise)
{
    perceivedExpertise <- sin(2*pi*actualExpertise)*DK_
    SkewParameter/(2*pi) + actualExpertise
    return(perceivedExpertise);
}


    initialize_confidence <- function(individualId) {
    numberOfConnections <- 5
    mat_row <- matrix(0,num_participants,1)
    candidateNeighbourIds <- (1:num_participants)[-individualId];
    indexOfNeighbours <- sample(candidateNeighbourIds,
    numberOfConnections);
    confidence <- runif(numberOfConnections);
    mat_row[indexOfNeighbours] <- confidence;
    return(mat_row)
}
initialize_expertise <- function()
{
    expertise <- runif(num_participants)
    return(expertise)
}
castVotes <- function(vote_transfers)
{
    #Everyone has 1 vote in the beginning
    vote_vector <- c()
    vote_vector[1:num_participants] <- 1
    summation_term <- matrix(0, num_participants, num_
    participants)
    vote_transfers.diag <- diag(diag(vote_transfers)) #diag(diag())
    because we want a matrix
```

```r
weight <- 1
for (k in 0:num_participants) {
    vote_transfers.updated <- vote_transfers - vote_transfers.
    diag
    vote_transfers.updated <- vote_transfers.updated %^% k
    vote_transfers.updated <- vote_transfers.updated *
    weight

    summation_term <- summation_term + vote_transfers.
    updated
}


    transfer_result <- vote_transfers.diag %*% summation_term
    %*% vote_vector
    return(transfer_result);
}


#Deciding on where votes get transfered based on expertise/trust
initialize_voteTransfer <- function(expertise,conf_matrix){
    vote_transfers <- matrix(0,num_participants,num_participants)
    for (i in 1:num_participants) {
    # This is the greatest expertise among the individual's trusted
    network
    # after passing through the DK effect
    max_exp <- max(
        c(dunningKrugerEffect(expertise[conf_matrix[i,] >
        minimumconfidence]),
            -1))

        #If the potential proxy's expertise is greater than the
        individuals', transfer
        if (max_exp > 0 &&
            dunningKrugerEffect(expertise[i]) < max_exp) {
                transfer_index <- match(max_exp, expertise)
                vote_transfers[transfer_index,i] <- 1
    }
    else {
        vote_transfers[i,i] <- 1
    }
    }
    return(vote_transfers);
}
```

```r
holdProxyElection <- function()
{
    conf_matrix <- t(sapply(1:num_participants, initialize_
    confidence))
    expertise <- initialize_expertise();
    vote_transfers <- initialize_voteTransfer(expertise,conf_matrix)
    transfer_result <- castVotes(vote_transfers)
    expertVotes <- getExpertVotes(expertise,transfer_result)

    return(list(transfer_result= transfer_result,expertVotes =
    expertVotes))
}

getExpertVotes <- function(expertise, transfer_result)
{
    p_abs_maj <- c()
    totalVotingPower <- sum(transfer_result)
    if(totalVotingPower==0)
    {
        return(matrix(0,length(minimumExpertise),1));
    }
    for (exp_level in minimumExpertise) {
        experts <- (expertise > exp_level)

        maj_sum <- sum(transfer_result[experts])/totalVotingPower
        maj_sum <- 100*(maj_sum > 0.5)
        p_abs_maj <- c(p_abs_maj, maj_sum)
    }
    return(p_abs_maj)
}

simulateMultipleProxyElections <- function(numberOfRuns=1e3)
{
    result_matrix <- NULL
    for(i in 1:numberOfRuns)
    {
        #Keep track of results over all runs
        proxyElectionResults <- holdProxyElection()
        result_matrix <- rbind(result_matrix,
                                proxyElectionResults["expertVotes"]
                                [[1]])
    }
    return(result_matrix)
}
```

```r
createPlot <- function(simulationData,figId = NULL)
{
    numberOfRuns <- dim(simulationData)[1]
    probabilities <- colMeans(simulationData)
    stdDeviations <- apply(simulationData, 2, sd)/
    sqrt(numberOfRuns)*3
    lowerConfidenceBound <- probabilities-stdDeviations
    upperConfidenceBound <- probabilities+stdDeviations

    plot(minimumExpertise, probabilities, ylim=c(0,100),
        type="l", main=figId,
        xlab="Minimum expertise required to solve problem",
        ylab="Probability of absolute majority")
    lines(minimumExpertise, lowerConfidenceBound,
    lty="dashed", type="l", col="red")
    lines(minimumExpertise, upperConfidenceBound,
    lty="dashed", type="l", col="red")

    #Ovelaying graph of expertise-based democracy
    democracyProbabilities <- 100*sapply(minimumExpertise,
    function(x)1-pbinom(num_participants/2,num_participants,1-x))
    lines(minimumExpertise,democracyProbabilities,type="l",
    col="blue")
    legend("bottomleft",legend = c
            ("Proxy voting","Lower confidence-bound","upper
                confidence-bound","Direct voting"),
        fill=c("black","red","red","blue"),cex=.7)
}

# Variable name syntax: 'simulationResults_' + PERCENTAGE_
TRUST +'_' + DK_SKEW_PARAMETER_VALUE
simulationResults_60_0 <- simulateMultipleProxyElections()

DK_SkewParameter <- 2
simulationResults_60_2 <- simulateMultipleProxyElections();

minimumconfidence <- .8
DK_SkewParameter <- 0
simulationResults_80_0 <- simulateMultipleProxyElections()

DK_SkewParameter <- 2
simulationResults_80_2 <- simulateMultipleProxyElections()
```

```
minimumconfidence <- .95
DK_SkewParameter <- 0
simulationResults_95_0 <- simulateMultipleProxyElections()

DK_SkewParameter <- 2
simulationResults_95_2 <- simulateMultipleProxyElections()
```

www.ingramcontent.com/pod-product-compliance
Lightning Source LLC
Chambersburg PA
CBHW070932260726
48661CB00003B/961